Canada and the Global Economy

Robert Chodos, Rae Murphy,
and Eric Hamovitch

James Lorimer & Company, Publishers
Toronto, 1993

James Lorimer & Company Ltd. acknowledges with thanks the support of the Canada Council, the Ontario Arts Council and the Ontario Publishing Centre in the development of writing and publishing in Canada.

Canadian Cataloguing in Publication Data
  Chodos, Robert, 1947-
    Canada and the global economy

Includes bibliographical references and index.
ISBN 1-55028-418-5 (bound) ISBN 1-55028-419-3 (pbk.)

1. Canada - Commercial policy. 2. Canada - Economic policy - 1991- .* 3. Canada - Economic conditions - 1991 - .* 4. Economic forecasting - Canada. I. Murphy, Rae, 1935 - . II. Hamovitch, Eric. III. Title.

HC113.C48 1993   382'.3'0971 C93-093837-2

James Lorimer & Company Ltd., Publishers
35 Britain Street
Toronto, Ontario M5A 1R7

Printed and bound in Canada

Contents

Chapter 1

The New World Order and Canada's Place in It

The term *globalization* has become the economic and political mantra of our time. Just repeat it and economic movements and phenomena are explained. Unemployment here, an agricultural trade war there, a massive leveraged buyout yonder, a staggering bankruptcy under our unsuspecting noses — someone will inevitably say these are merely the consequences of "global economic restructuring" or just plain "globalization." The term is so widely used that it is often rendered meaningless.

Yet something profound is changing the world's economic, political and social reality. Neither the globalization of trade nor the apparently contradictory growth of exclusive trading blocs is particularly new, but recent technology that permits instantaneous communication and a global capital marketplace has changed the scale and pace of economic activity across national borders. There is also a fundamental change in the nature of trade itself. Historically, nation-states — and city-states before them — exchanged different goods with different peoples.

The problem with world trade now is that everybody — or almost everybody — makes and attempts to sell the same things. Where once no one would ever attempt to carry coals to Newcastle, the Japanese not only carry cars to Detroit but actually make thousands there for export back to Japan. Exotic cargoes from the Orient are now more likely to be computer chips and high-tech components of every description.

Global trade is now a mélange of competition and cooperation, joint ventures and fierce struggles for market share. Consider the archcompetitors in the aerospace industry: the American giant Boeing and the European Airbus consortium. Boeing is the supposed paradigm of a free-market venture and, incidentally, the largest single source of foreign revenues in the United States. Airbus is not only state-backed and -controlled, but a cooperative effort of several European governments.

The two companies are studying ways to cooperate on the development of the superjumbo jet, while at the same time both forge ahead with their individual designs for similar aircraft. In the automobile industry, while American manufacturers scream for access to the Japanese market, there is significant American investment in the Japanese firms that have held tremendous North American market share. American and Japanese companies forge any number of alliances and joint ventures.

It is too early to pinpoint the profound social implications of these changes. We can, however, see the truth in Richard J. Barnet and Ronald E. Müller's 1974 study of the modern multinational corporation, *Global Reach*, in which they described the managers of these corporations as "the first to have developed a plausible model of the future that is global. They exploit the advantages of mobility while workers and governments are still tied to particular territories. For this reason, the corporate visionaries are far ahead of the rest of the world in making claims on the future. In making business decisions today they are creating a politics for the next generation."[1]

In more recent writings, Barnet illustrates this new global reality: "No national government can control the huge amounts of capital that travel across the world via computer; twenty-four hours a day, every day, more than five hundred billion dollars flows through the world's major foreign-exchange markets beyond the control of any regulation."[2] He thus warns against any attempt by the United States to lapse into isolationism or into some sort of protectionist trade war. However, it may be more than just premature to see the world as one vast holding company, as envisioned by American film writer Paddy Chayefsky in his brilliant 1976 satire *Network*. Rather, the process of "globalization" may really be a realignment of the world into mutually exclusive economic units that will gaze with hostility at one another at the close of our century just as the old empires did at the century's dawn.

As the only current superpower,[3] the United States is conceded to have national interests, but it does not have the power to protect these interests except by going with the flow. Barnet mentions "the great engines of the American economy" and concludes, "[No] national government can control them, much less force them to serve a nationalistic policy that they do not perceive to be in their own interest."

Countries are now more or less powerless to control their own currency and thus their own fiscal, monetary and, therefore, economic policy. By "more or less," we mean that weaker states with minor currencies, such as Canada, have less control than Germany or the United States, for example. But even dominant powers find that their capacity to achieve the economic outcomes they desire is constrained to a much greater extent than it used to be. Thus, high German interest rates virtually destroyed the concept of a single European currency and forced a devaluation of the weaker currencies in Europe. But Germany was not immune from the effects of this policy: the Bundesbank could not devise a way to mitigate the German recession, which has now spread to the rest of Europe. In the United States, President Bill Clinton's economic reforms cannot be implemented without the consent of the Japanese, among others. The American administration wants to replace free trade with strategic trade, a useful euphemism for an activist government operating within an industrial policy, and the Japanese simply refuse to play any longer by American rules — old or new.

All nation-states are under pressure and threatened in their real historic role — the capacity to create and control a domestic market. Yet nothing has arisen to replace the nation-state in this role. The former dream of a borderless world of prosperity, peace and freedom, brought to us by the threat or promise of the one universal holding company, has been replaced by visions of the absolute anarchy of the capital market. The "virtual corporation" meets the virtual economy.

With changing concepts of sovereignty and the real restrictions being placed on all state power by international trade agreements, the question is what will emerge to defend the economic and social interests of society as a whole as distinct from the interests of international capital. This also involves issues of the distribution of wealth within a given country and, perhaps of more significance, among the regions of the world.

Starting in about 1980, the destruction of the so-called welfare state and the entrenchment of a neoconservative agenda became dominant themes in the politics of Britain, the United States and Canada. However, this has not been the main political or economic thrust of the more successful European governments, and the activist state or superstate has been the hallmark of the march towards economic union in Europe. Interventionism also characterizes the state polices of Japan and several of the emerging "tigers" of Asia —

notably South Korea, Taiwan and Singapore. In North America, free trade agreements accompanied by economic deregulation, less government economic and social involvement, and sustained attacks on living standards in the name of competition are presented as the irresistible wave of the future. However, those economies that have thrived in this new era have followed very different policies.

In the fall of 1991, highly skilled and paid employees of the giant agricultural implement manufacturer Caterpillar, in the American heartland of Peoria, Illinois, went on strike. These workers were earning lower real wages than in the 1970s and their standard of living had declined. But the strike was a defensive one by the union to protect their conditions. Donald V. Fites, chair of Caterpillar, told a New York *Times* interviewer that American incomes should tread water while those of other countries should catch up: "There is a narrowing gap between the average American's income and that of the Mexican's. As a human being, I think what is going on is positive." More to the point than Fites's opinions as a human being is the fact that as head of Caterpillar he is pursuing a strategy (a successful one, according to recent reports[4]) leading to the relative impoverishment of his employees. Yes, it is important for the income of Mexico's workers to catch up to that of workers in the United States and Canada, as we argue in defending the principle — if not the details — of the North American Free Trade Agreement. But there is a difference between favouring greater equity among the three NAFTA partners and using the threat of Mexican competition to drive down wages and working conditions in Canada and the United States — a "race to the bottom" in which there are no winners.

People in Canada and elsewhere are told ever more frequently that changes in world trade, with the term *globalization* used as a sort of shorthand, will mean they have to choose between becoming more competitive to maintain a standard of living and accepting lower standards of living. These changes reflect the imperatives of economic growth and technical innovation, and they are directed, or so it often seems, by a handful of white or Japanese males at the pinnacles of corporate power with little regard for the effects on workers, communities, entire countries or, for that matter, the planet. This phenomenon takes on an aura of inevitability, which in turn creates a sense of disempowerment among many workers and communities.

Free Trade: A Canadian Conundrum

We hope to show in these pages how a different kind of internationalist perspective can help us take steps to steer globalization in a direction that reflects broader interests. Hardships lie ahead whether or not Canadians accept globalization, and it is difficult to see how globalization will go away just because some people would prefer not to accept it. We think an approach that is more hopeful — and that could even be feasible — lies in attempting, instead, to redirect the course of globalization.

We are also often reminded of the importance of increasing productivity. It has become axiomatic that only by increasing productivity can we raise our standard of living. It is worth noting that productivity has its flip side, which is unemployment. Productivity, by definition, depends on achieving higher production without adding more workers. Everyone can stay happy as long as markets are growing and sales rise enough to keep pace with productivity growth, but if sales stagnate or decline, then workers have to settle for shorter hours or, more commonly, layoffs, to keep sacrosanct productivity from dropping. Many factories have worked during the recession at much less than full capacity, which means they can get big potential production increases while hiring only a few additional workers. That is why we hear talk of a jobless recovery which, for the unemployed, means a recoveryless recovery. Modern economic history teaches us that employment does tend eventually to catch up to higher productivity, but for millions of workers in North America and elsewhere the wait is painfully long. This is one example of the way in which the pursuit of economic goals can prove socially regressive. We believe that, even or perhaps especially in the context of a global economy, there are times when social goals ought to come first.

Globalization poses particular problems and challenges for Canada — particular but in no way unique.

In many of the valedictories to Brian Mulroney in early 1993, the trite and unlikely notion that history will be a kinder judge of the outgoing prime minister than current public opinion was raised. In particular, the idea that his North American free trade crusade placed him firmly on the side of history was put forward. One pundit wrote that the perceptive PM realized that Canada could "no longer hide amid the ice-floes ... to find yet another way to continue to defy economics and geography."[5]

What defiance of economics and geography? Canada has, throughout its history, depended on foreign trade. Even when imprisoned within the colonial mercantile system, Canada's trading vessels coursed the Atlantic southward and eastward. Canadians always favoured any system of genuine reciprocity with the United States — or one that managed trade to their advantage such as the Auto Pact. They knew that it was vital to their own economic interests. Unlike the United States, or for that matter most of developed Europe, Canada has never enjoyed or been able to rely on an economically viable domestic market. Even the old National Policy, which was a direct response to the abrogation of a free trade agreement by the United States, was designed to create an internationally competitive trading economy — and it was magnificently successful. As former finance minister Michael Wilson never tired of pointing out, Canada is the world's eighth-largest economy and thirty-first largest population. Throughout its entire history Canada has lived in some sort of formal or informal economic association with the United States, Britain, the Commonwealth and Empire.

However, when it comes to much of the current usage, things are not always what they seem to be or are said to be. Indeed, the current Canada-U.S. Free Trade Agreement, which is in force even though one of its key elements, a subsidy code, remains unnegotiated, is not in the conventional sense a free trade agreement. It is designed to create a formal trading bloc to protect the domestic American market from the pressures of global trade represented by the Japanese and the Europeans. Globalization thus comes to Canada on the wings of a trading bloc in which it is about to be totally submerged. This has meant a retreat from world trade, from any independent role within the world system, into the exclusive bosom of the U.S. Thus, Canadian exports to the United States increased by more than $20 billion between 1988 and 1992; Canadian exports to the rest of the world actually declined slightly.[6]

With all the propaganda, special pleading, dire warnings and patronizing claptrap about the new "global village," the issue is not one of protectionists who seek somehow to hide from the world or even the continent versus the bold free traders. One can be a free trader and yet oppose the unbridled monopolist pressures that go to create a continental "division of labour" and replace Canada as an independent entity with a Canada that is fragmented into regional entities in a supercontinental — read American — market. While globalization does not exclude the absorption of Canada into the United States, or its becoming merely a spoke on the great wheel of Manifest Destiny, it does not make such a development inevitable. The consolidation of relatively exclusive trading blocs, on the other hand, would in fact make Canada's disappearance inevitable or at least the continuance of the appearance of a state irrelevant.

With Canada an appendage of the United States, economic integration increases the pressures for complete absorption. This is particularly the case in English Canada — more precisely Ontario — as the traditional Quebec-Ontario axis seems less and less relevant (total Quebec-Ontario trade in 1989 was barely a sixth of Canada-U.S. trade[7]) and the logic, at least on the surface, seems to make the concept of what U.S. State Department official Michael Vlahos calls USCAN, a merger of the two countries, inevitable and even desirable.[8] This is particularly true if one sees the world moving towards more or less stable trading blocs: Europe, America and Asia, in effect huge superstates. The magnetic power of the strong would naturally force adhesion of the weak. In Europe, history, culture and the large number of players in the European Community help mitigate this force of attraction; in North America, these mitigating factors are much weaker.

The U.S. is incomparably stronger and more centralized than Canada, but the concept of globalization implies a world in which no borders are sacrosanct. Even in the United States, federalism is under immense centrifugal pressures, not least of which is an attraction to the rising power and investment clout of Japan and the Asian tigers. For Canada, where Mike Harcourt's first out-of-province visit as premier of British Columbia was to Japan, Pacific trade is both vital today and promising for the future. Japan is B.C.'s second-largest trading partner, and about 25 per cent of B.C.'s trade is with the Pacific Rim. Trade with Ontario is down to single digits.

Free trade can mean — or not mean — many different things. It can mean that a small country such as Canada gets swallowed by a powerful neighbour that dominates a regional trading bloc, or it can mean that small countries take their rightful place in a setting of full multilateral free trade. We argue in favour of the latter outcome while suggesting ways to mitigate the effects of the former. And we assert that the interests of justice are not served by keeping obstacles in the way of trade with Mexico.

We endeavour to avoid buzzwords such as *managed trade,* which is a polite term for your neighbour's attempts to protect certain industries, or *fair trade,* which is what you call your own such attempts. The concept of a "level playing field" is interesting because it has the potential to eliminate international trade altogether: if a particular country insists it will open its markets only to others whose handicaps are just the same as its own, then it will have no one to trade with at all. Some anti-free-traders in the U.S. have said the North American Free Trade Agreement should be ratified only when Mexican wages approach U.S. levels;[9] Mexican protectionists could then argue that NAFTA should be ratified only when productivity levels in the two countries come closer. It is clear where such arguments can lead. Some Canadian opponents of the earlier bilateral agreement with the U.S. said Canadian agriculture would be wiped out under free trade because the U.S. has a longer growing season. If Americans slapped higher tariffs on imports of Canadian farm products because this country's rainfall is more favourable, the result would approach autarky (absolute self-sufficiency). In the real world of trade, there is no such thing as a level playing field. Producing something where it is advantageous to do so and selling it in a place that does not share those advantages is the very essence of trade.

But while avoiding such buzzwords as *managed trade* and the *level playing field,* we will have occasion to refer to the Law of Unintended Consequences. This law is based on the observation that a course of action undertaken in the hope and devout belief that it will produce a particular outcome often ends up leading to a very different one. Thus, the United States built up the Japanese economy after the Second World War because it wanted to keep Japan in the anti-Communist fold. In the process it helped create a serious economic rival whose success as an exporter would contribute to the decay of much of the industrial U.S. Northeast and Midwest. Canada wanted an open economy, good relations with the United States and something approaching American-style prosperity. In pursuing these goals it has reached the point where, as we will show, its continued existence as a sovereign entity is problematic. Countries often find it especially difficult to deal with situations that arise through the operation of the Law of Unintended Consequences because they are not part of the script.

The Law of Unintended Consequences helps resolve one of the chief paradoxes of globalization. On the one hand, globalization is a human phenomenon proceeding from human decisions. On the other, it appears as a natural force that cannot be stopped. Globalization is actually in large measure a product of the unintended consequences of human decisions. It was, perhaps, intended by the corporations that have been its chief beneficiaries (although even companies such as IBM have not been immune from its unintended consequences), but it was facilitated by governments pursuing other goals: progress and prosperity. Unless we are willing to give up on those goals, globalization (or its bastard, regional trading blocs) is here to stay. We remain optimistic that it can be rechannelled in a more socially beneficial direction, but first it must be understood.

In the following chapters, we look first at what globalization is and is not, and also at an earlier internationalism that owed more to Karl Marx than to the Fortune 500. We touch on the links between economic and military strategy, the development of the international monetary system, and the nature of sovereignty and nationalism in a changing world. We also look at the efforts of some contemporary groups, especially in the areas of health and the environment, to build international networks in an effort to form a counterweight to multinational corporations and their allies.

Later we examine the growth of the European Community and of trade blocs in other parts of the world with particular emphasis on NAFTA, while pointing to the advantages of a multilateral approach to trade liberalization that spans rather than separates the continents. Then we discuss control of Canada's economic destiny with examinations of the automobile, steel and airline industries. And, with special emphasis on agriculture, we urge a conceptual separation of trade and social policy so that each can be put on a more solid footing. Finally, we examine the cultural implications of globalization.

We hope to show that freer trade is not inherently something to be feared and resisted. Rather, it can be made into an opportunity to deal with corporate power and pursue social progress on a worldwide rather than merely a national basis as part of a new internationalism.

Chapter 2

How New Is Globalization?

Until comparatively recent times, most of the world's trade consisted of exchanges within small localities. In the emerging great civilizations of the eastern Mediterranean and China, and then later in medieval Europe, in the colonial societies of the Western hemisphere and even recently in some of the less accessible reaches of Asia and Africa, individual towns and villages maintained only limited commercial ties with the outside world; most of what they consumed was produced locally.

Communities that built the most elaborate trading networks also tended to be among the most prosperous. They had access to a wider variety of goods and could choose the ones that offered the finest quality or the lowest cost. They also had more potential customers for their own products and could sell to those who bid the highest price. Even so, the time and the cost of transport meant that long-distance trade in basic goods usually didn't pay, which is partly why early travel accounts speak so often of luxuries such as silks and spices.

In the eighteenth and nineteenth centuries, the nature of trade was transformed by two fundamental developments. The consolidation of the nation-state in Europe as the basic unit of political organization altered the notion of community and refocused the concept of sovereignty. In addition, the advent of steamships and railways meant that goods could be shipped more quickly and more cheaply over longer distances.

The sovereign nation-state did not spring to life all at once. Ideas of national sovereignty had provided French kings from the sixteenth century onward with the moral authority to challenge rebellious feudal barons in the name of a higher good. Later on, eighteenth-century philosophers such as Jean-Jacques Rousseau developed the notion of governments exercising sovereignty in the name of the people. The revolutions that swept Europe from 1789 to

1848 eliminated many vestiges of feudalism and spurred the development of national states, a process that reached its culmination late in the nineteenth century with the forging of the German and Italian states.

British historian Eric Hobsbawm writes of the period between 1789 and 1848 as that of the dual revolutions: the French Revolution and the contemporaneous British industrial revolution. It was the triumph not of "industry" as such but of capitalist industry; not of liberty and equality in general but of middle-class or "bourgeois" liberal society; not of the "modern economy" or the "modern state" but the economies and states in a particular geographical region (part of Europe and a few patches of North America) whose centre was the neighbouring and rival states of Great Britain and France. The transformation of 1789–1848 is essentially the twin upheaval that took place in those countries and was propagated thence across the entire world.

As the capitalist nation-state developed and became consolidated and the national market was entrenched, the interests of the market and those of the nation appeared to be coterminous. The expansion of European and North American capitalist interests into new territories in Africa, Asia and Latin America only reinforced this perception.[1] It was only a) when the process of colonialism was more or less complete and when the first incipient colonial revolutions began to occur; b) when newer European powers began to emerge and seek "Lebensraum" (living space); and c) when Japan rose to challenge European and American hegemony that the political limitations, indeed dangers, of the nation-state and concepts of narrow nationalism began to manifest themselves. It was somewhat later that the contradiction between the oneness — the globalization — of the world economy and the sovereignty and regulatory functions of the nation-state, its colonies and spheres became apparent.

This was in part merely a delay in perception. Even in the nineteenth century, markets did not end at national borders and there are many examples of international cartels and market divisions that could surive any transnational political crisis. The Rothschilds had become "international" before 1800, and a good deal of the foundation of their British wealth was due to signals sent them by their European cousins about the outcome of the battle of Waterloo in 1815, allowing them a full twenty-four hours to buy undervalued British bonds. While nationalist movements in Europe often impeded the development of the European economy, there were also constant counterpressures, beginning with free trade measures and other international treaties that facilitated the movement of goods. Hobsbawm describes various mid-nineteenth-century international agreements to devlop free or at least liberalized trade relations and concludes that "the question of what part institutional or legal changes play in fostering or hindering economic development is too complex for the simple mid-nineteenth-century formula: 'liberalization creates economic progress.'"[2]

Real historical events, especially in the twentieth century, also helped mask the contradiction between the existence of the nation-state and the new world market. The first major war for the redistribution of power resulted in the removal of the Russian Empire and the subsequent creation of a Communist bloc of nations and a capitalist bloc. This fact was basic to the militant nationalism and the political and military power of the superstates that has characterized most of this century.

Describing the revolutionary aspect of modern capitalism, Marx and Engels wrote:

> A single unconscionable freedom — Free Trade — . . . [has] given a cosmopolitan character to production and consumption in every country. . . . All old-established national industries have been destroyed or are daily being destroyed. . . . In place of the old local and national seclusion and self-sufficiency, we have intercourse in every direction, universal interdependence of nations. And as in material, so also in intellectual creations. The intellectual creations of individual nations become common property.[3]

But tempestuous growth, what the economist Joseph Schumpeter described as "creative destruction," which is the revolutionary hallmark of capitalism, came off the rails when national rivalries spilled over into war in 1914. With the return of Russia and its surrounding countries to the fold, it is now more or less back on the rails. We are set to resume the course towards economic integration that was laid out when the Congress of Vienna stabilized Europe in 1814–15 and continued without significant interruption through the rest of the nineteenth century. Now, however, there can be no question of the market's being served by the consolidation of the nation-state. Now the perception — and, at least in part, the fact — is that the nation-state is not only being eroded by the development of the forces it unleashed and nourished but actually stands in contradiction to the further development of those forces. Central to any discussion of globalization is the question of how that contradiction is to be resolved.

Lenin and the Global Economy

The Economist began a special report on multinational corporations in early 1993 with reference to a work by V.I. Lenin, founder of the Soviet state, in which he characterized the export of capital as not only a distinctive phase of capitalism but its final phase.[4] The magazine noted the irony of the collapse of Communism coinciding with the years 1983–90 in which foreign investment grew four times faster than world output and three times faster than world trade. Even though the "boom has faded in recession-hit industrial countries . . . foreign investment is rushing enthusiastically to those countries that for decades were blighted by communism."

This presumably is irony number two although, perhaps to make the "rushing enthusiastically" sound less preposterous than it is, the writers widened Lenin's blight to include "China, India, other parts of Asia, Latin America and even Eastern Europe." Not to be churlish, we might suggest that the countries listed were hardly economic paradises before Lenin took power in the rotted hulk of the Czarist empire and that, in any case, his influence over most of those mentioned was minimal. However, let us agree with *The Economist* that "not for the first time, Lenin's analysis missed the mark."

But what was his analysis? And how far from the mark? And how could this possibly relate to today's world economic and trading patterns? This, in our minds, is irony number three, the one *The Economist* missed.

The book of Lenin's in question is *Imperialism: The Highest Stage of Capitalism*, which he wrote while he was in exile in Zürich in 1916. The First World War was grinding to a murderous stalemate, and Lenin, one of the more obscure Social Democratic world luminaries but certainly the most important leader of the fragmented movement in Russia, was conducting a lonely war against the war. The powerful Social Democratic parties in Europe had supported the various war efforts of their countries.

As the Russian army began to collapse and the fragile economy buckled, a revolution broke out in Petrograd, the capital, and other regions of the empire. The German general staff either realized or were convinced that Lenin could do more harm to the Russian war effort in Petrograd than in Zürich. Lenin and several associates were quickly bundled into a sealed train and carried back to Petrograd. On arrival in the city, Lenin was greeted as a hero and he quickly seized the initiative by mounting a tank (just as a later Russian leader was to do) and proceeding to do exactly what the Germans wanted him to do. That Lenin's antiwar crusade was part of his overall revolutionary strategy concerned the German general staff not at all.

Although at the time one event had nothing to do with the other, Lenin's book, or at least the theory postulated in it, would later serve to justify the appropriateness of making a separate peace and presuming to organize a Communist revolution in a country such as Russia. It would later still, and much more tenuously, provide some of the theoretical justification for the un-Marxist concept of building socialism in a single country, whose implementation under Stalin would fatally undermine the internationalism that had characterized the Communist movement.

In the rush of events between its publication and his death in 1924, Lenin had little time for *Imperialism*, and neither, for that matter, did anyone else. Lenin saw it mainly as a polemic against leaders of the Social Democratic movements of Europe who supported the war and who now supported the "Wilsonian" peace of Versailles. As Lenin freely acknowledged, most of the observations, conclusions and supporting arguments in the book were actually the work of a British pacifist and social democrat, J.A. Hobson, and to a lesser extent that of the German Social Democratic leader Rudolf Hilferding. Hobson in particular linked imperialism with the massive export of capital as the basis of the modern European empires — the new colonialism. Hobson's work was published in the very early years of the century when the worldwide demand for capital was insatiable.

Imperial Russia was the target for much of this investment, especially from France and Britain. Russian capitalism had a number of peculiarities, which Lenin and others noted. Its fundamental weakness was that it depended almost totally on Western investment, and Russia was thus sucked into a devastating war on the side of the Entente that in no way reflected its interests and for which it was completely unprepared. Capitalism in Russia was also unique in that the state was a major player. The so-called market operated within a state structure based on tariffs, concessions and direct financial control.[5] The demands of the war, combined with the fragile infrastructure of a state in transition from a feudal autocracy to an uncertain modernity, created the conditions for a revolution, which Lenin described as occurring when the ruling classes cannot govern in the same way and the masses of people cannot continue to live in the same way.

If the particular conditions of wartime Russia convinced Lenin that a revolutionary situation existed, it was the nature of modern capitalism itself that made a successful revolution possible: a world revolution that breaks the system at its weakest link. Lenin thus made the connection between "imperialism" and Marx's notions of the uneven development of capitalism between various countries and regions. A global economy had developed within and around regional and national disparities in the context of competition for markets and capital investment opportunities. The 1913 economic recession made the issue less the expansion of the global economy than its redistribution. It was the redistribution of the existing market, now saturated and in a period of contraction, that led to the world war.

Lenin also used these observations to conclude that the most successful powers could use part of the superprofits they made from exploiting the underdeveloped and unsuccessful economies to the advantage of their own people. This, of course, clobbered the theories of the early economists such as Malthus and Ricardo, and even did violence to Marx's understanding of the workings of the system and the impoverishment of the working class. It also helped explain how even the dispossessed could identify with the imperial interests of "their" capitalists and "their" nation. The workers of all lands, and especially the wealthiest capitalist lands, had much more to lose than their chains.

However, the old global economy, like its successors, was unable to abolish the economic cycle. This was expressed eloquently by *The Economist*:

The reason why he [Lenin] bothered to comment on foreign investment was that trade and cross-border investment also boomed in 1870–1913. . . . The world economy approached integration at an even faster pace than seen in the past forty years. . . . Most of the world took part in a monetary union called the gold standard. . . . [Migration made] the labour market more integrated. Yet this did not lead to a global Utopia. It was brought to an end by a set of non-tariff barriers and regulatory obstacles called the first world war, which were followed by tariff barriers of the 1920s and 1930s.

> So far the current boom . . . has been interrupted by something
> as mundane as a recession.[6]

We believe the operative words here are *so far*. After all, *The Economist* did not have to end its historical throwaway lines with the 1930s.
After the Depression came that other great non-tariff barrier, the
Second World War. Then there was the new monetary union called
the Bretton Woods agreement.

Lenin saw the world as moving towards one integral economy,
which as we have seen meant that the capitalist system could snap
under stress at its weakest link. The stress was the war, and the weak
link was Russia. When it became clear that Russia did not inspire
the world revolution, Lenin became much more tentative in his
approach. As soon as the civil war was decided, Lenin moved to a
New Economic Policy, which encouraged the development of a
limited market system. As brief as it was, the NEP period in Russia
saw a freer market than the one that had existed under the czar. The
NEP also encouraged foreign investment and on the whole was not
unlike the economic and political reforms Mikhail Gorbachev tried
to implement.

Whether Lenin's or Gorbachev's reforms could have saved the
system, or what that system would have become, is impossible to
guess. Lenin, it seems, did not hold out much hope. Eric Hobsbawm
tells how Lenin, who saw the Russian revolution as the successor to
the Paris Commune (which, never mind one country, appeared to
think of socialism in one city), counted the days the Commune had
lasted — less than two months.[7] When the time passed he announced
triumphantly: "We have outlasted the Commune!" What the nature,
circumstances and duration of the next experiment in building a
society based on something other than profit and competition will be
is, again, impossible to guess. But it might be prudent to adopt some
of *The Economist*'s cautionary language and say that Lenin has been
proven wrong, so far.

Remembering P.I.

Before we put Lenin back in the historical dustbin to which he has
been consigned since the late 1980s, it is worth taking a look at
another idea that he held dear: proletarian internationalism. This term
is a marketing nightmare. It has far too many syllables, and to the
uninitiated it may have a vaguely menacing ring, especially after the

aggressive way it was brandished by Trotskyist groups of yore. But the mere mention of proletarian internationalism (let's call it P.I. for short) should serve as a reminder of something that seems largely to escape notice in the continuing debate over free trade — namely that the barons of capitalism are not the only group this century that has striven to surmount national barriers. Internationalism is by no means the exclusive heritage of the corporate sector or its political allies. As hard as it may be to imagine these days, leftists and liberals have at times been more internationalist in outlook than their adversaries on the right.

Today's internationalist buzzword, *globalization,* has been marketed far more effectively than P.I. ever was, helped in large measure by the fact that the concept it denotes is closer to reality. The process of globalization consists of erasing national borders in the production and distribution of goods and services. As currently practised, it contains the clear understanding that those who are unable or unwilling to compete are going to get left behind. This message gets repeated so often as to appear inevitable, and this in turn is being used to disempower trade unions and intimidate critics of corporate power. It need not be thus.

The "proletarian" version of internationalism (which in any case badly needs updating) has little in common with the current corporate version. The two are not directly in competition today, and this has much to do with the virtual abdication of the political left, which in its more vigorous moments seems more intent on trying to derail a train that has already gone past than on signalling ahead to switch it to a different track.

Now that Marxism and its associated vocabulary have fallen so deeply out of fashion, we hear little mention of the international working class. But as Marx saw it, when the heightening of contradictions between labour and capital created revolutionary pressures, working people in advanced capitalist societies would find more in common with one another than with their respective national bourgeoisies. Lenin developed this line of thinking with the following comments in 1913:

> Working-class democracy contraposes to the nationalist wrangling of the various bourgeois parties . . . the demand for the unconditional unity and complete amalgamation of workers of all nationalities in all working-class organizations — trade union, cooperative, consumers', educational and all others — in

contradistinction to any kind of bourgeois nationalism. Only this type of unity and amalgamation can uphold democracy and defend the interests of the workers against capital — which is already international and is becoming more so — and promote the development of mankind towards a new way of life that is alien to all privileges and all exploitation.[8]

Lenin's comments here were directed to the situation inside Russia with its myriad minority nationalities and their mutual distrust, but his reference to the international nature of capital suggests a broader scope. Rendered in the jargon of today, these lines could send a strong message even now. Further on, Lenin quotes disparagingly from an article by a Mr. F. Liebman in a publication of the Marxist but non-Bolshevik Jewish workers' Bund:

Anyone in the least familiar with the national question knows that international culture is not nonnational culture (culture without a national form); nonnational culture, which must not be Russian, Jewish or Polish but only pure culture, is nonsense; international ideas can appeal to the working class only when they are adapted to the language spoken by the worker and to the concrete national conditions under which he [*sic*] lives.[9]

Again, eight decades later, we encounter a powerful resonance. Lenin and Liebman had engaged the thorny issue of the relationship between culture and economics, which is inescapable in the free trade controversies of today. Replace "Russian, Jewish or Polish" with "American, Canadian or Mexican" and we have stepped straight into the NAFTA debate — or rather into themes the NAFTA debate ought to be examining.

Needless to say, Liebman's argument did not go unanswered. "The national culture of the bourgeoisie is a fact," Lenin railed. "Aggressive bourgeois nationalism, which drugs the minds of the workers, stultifies and disunites them in order that the bourgeoisie may lead them by the halter — such is the fundamental fact of the times. Those who seek to serve the proletariat must unite the workers of all nations and unswervingly fight bourgeois nationalism, domestic and foreign."[10]

Lenin addressed this message equally to the workers of oppressed nations, who in his eyes were especially vulnerable to the blandishments of national bourgeoisies that wished to divert their attention from the class struggle. National oppression must be fought not by bourgeois manipulation, but by workers of the oppressed and oppressor nations struggling side by side, he insisted. This is the essence of proletarian internationalism.

Words, words, words, and no more convincing coming from the pen of a soon-to-be leader of a past and future imperial state. As already noted, at the time of the First World War, P.I. was honoured mostly in the breach. And with the benefit of hindsight, we can see that what Chinese leader Mao Zedong would later denigrate as Soviet social imperialism meant that P.I. could be twisted to serve the interests of the Soviet Union generally and of the cynical manipulators in the Kremlin more specifically. Nevertheless, millions of people around the world, including many in Western countries, were convinced. They were drawn by the nobility of socialist ideals and buoyed by the early accomplishments of the Soviet state. Banners and speeches at labour rallies commonly urged workers of the world to unite, and this sense of international solidarity spread beyond Moscow-affiliated Communist circles to encompass a broad swath of the political left, with Trotskyist and social democratic parties forming their own Socialist Internationals.

Even during this heyday, it could not reliably be argued that working-class people in North America were notably more internationalist in outlook than other classes in society, except to the extent that many of them were immigrants. In fact, competition for jobs and housing was as likely to provoke xenophobia on the part of longer-established groups. But many organizations claiming to represent working people did at least pay lip service to internationalist principles.

If Lenin's words seem only semicomprehensible today, this has much to do with broad shifts in the way the class structure of modern capitalist societies is perceived. People at vastly different income levels and chasms apart in social status insist on being called middle-class, whether they be underpaid nurses or millionaire lawyers. Hardly anyone admits to being a plutocrat, and only those very low on the heap seem willing to accept the working-class label. For a middle class to exist there has to be something above and something below, but this obvious bit of logic has been obscured by the myth of a classless society. If there is no bourgeoisie and no proletariat, you can't very well engage in the Marxist-Leninist concept of class struggle (supposing, of course, that you want to). So you do what Bill Clinton did and promise the great majority of the middle class that you'll be nicer to them than to the people in some arbitrarily defined top tax brackets, thereby reversing the thrust of the version of class warfare engaged in by Ronald Reagan and George Bush (although they certainly wouldn't want you calling it that).

Labels come and go, but different elements in society continue to hold conflicting interests. These interests will continue to be promoted with greater or lesser success at the local, national and global levels. Multinational corporations know all about this and are less likely than other groups to suffer pangs of patriotism in pursuing their interests globally. Different groups, though, will waver when confronted with conflicts between group or class loyalty and national loyalty. For Lenin the choice was simple, but for others such as Liebman, the Bundist and Jewish nationalist, this was a more complex matter.

As noted above, Liebman argued that workers were deeply imbued with their national cultures and that there was no such thing as a nonnational culture. This remains true today. What some may regard in the narrow sense as international culture, in particular the output of Hollywood and its various adjuncts, has a clear national identity. This identity is American, and no less so for the fact that Hollywood has for decades not relied exclusively on American talent but drawn on the creative energies of many countries. That is the way it is with dominant cultures, and asking workers or others to give up part of their national identity in the interests of a higher solidarity would be to succumb to the dominant power. Culture in the more ample sense (to which Liebman obviously referred) encompasses much more than entertainment; it includes broad social and political perspectives. Are we to let these go as well?

Without getting too caught up in the debates of another era, we can give both Lenin and Liebman their due by stating that our own line of argument runs in favour of both international solidarity and a vibrant diversity of cultures. If it is not always possible to separate economics from culture in its broad sense, neither is it necessary to forsake the cultural values a country or region holds dear to establish closer cooperation across national boundaries.

A sensible internationalism most emphatically does not require groups of working people to be pitted against one another simply because they happen to live on different sides of a national boundary. The argument is made that a free flow of goods renders such conflict inevitable. We find it more plausible that closer international ties are the only way to *prevent* it from happening. Trade unions and their political allies in different countries can effectively oppose a ratcheting down of real wages and benefits only by working together and not by trying to isolate their national markets and thus protect the profit margins of national oligopolies. (This argument has begun to surface in some unlikely places. A May 1993 exchange of views in an obscure New York socialist publication called *The Militant* on whether opposing free trade is in the workers' interests included the following passage: "This perspective of hitching the fate of workers to the employers' profit goals is lethal for working people because it undermines our ability to act collectively and self-confidently and saps our solidarity by pitting workers of one industry, region, or country against another."[11])

It is easy to lose sight of the fact that, during the first two-thirds of the twentieth century, the forces of right-wing reaction, particularly in North America, were more likely than the left to toil in the causes of isolationism and protectionism, even when these impinged occasionally on the broad commercial interests of their fellows in big business.

Looking at the contemporary political panorama, we have seen Tories in Canada and Republicans in the U.S. championing agreements to promote freer trade with neighbouring countries and pushing for more open worldwide trade in services and farm products, while their opponents to the left scramble to justify continued barriers to trade. While Reagan, Bush and Mulroney laid the basis for what they promised would be the elimination of impediments to trade within North America, Canadian Liberals and NDPers, along with their allies among labour and social action groups, kicked up a storm in opposition. In the U.S., the new Clinton administration seemed uncertain in its early months which way it would tilt on fundamental trade issues, and the Democratic congressional leadership seemed frankly hostile towards the freer entry of imported goods. House Majority Leader Richard Gephardt, for one, has rarely seen a protectionist measure he did not like, and he is not alone.

There are sound reasons for this ideological alignment on the trade question, including well-founded suspicions stemming from the pro-corporate nature of the current internationalist agenda, but this represents a stunning reversal of the positions staked out earlier this century when Republicans and Conservatives were the parties of high tariffs. The Liberal Party of Canada lost the 1911 election on the question of reciprocal trade with the U.S. and was tagged as the party of continentalism long afterward. The Conservative Party, right up to the era of John Diefenbaker, preferred to lean on the British imperial tariff. Pierre Trudeau's nationalist tilt, followed by Mulroney's fulsome pro-Americanism, put a rapid reversal to that traditional alignment.

As usual, the U.S. took a more muscular approach, especially in the years between the two World Wars. That period opened with Senator Henry Cabot Lodge, the reactionary Republican blueblood from Massachusetts, leading the opposition to U.S. entry into the League of Nations as he sought to reimpose U.S. isolation from European affairs (while preserving Latin America as a playground for U.S. misadventures). It continued with a Republican-inspired tariff act in 1922 that hampered the ability of the defeated European countries of the First World War to meet their war reparations obligations.

Perhaps the sorriest moment occurred when, with great flourish, Republican President Herbert Hoover signed the Hawley-Smoot tariff act into law in 1930. That act raised tariffs sharply on a vast range of goods, including many that faced almost no import competition. Its authors were Republican senators noted for their rabid support of big business, and the measure they introduced spurred a frenzy of log-rolling in the two houses of Congress, both Republican-dominated, as member after member sought protection for industries in their districts and states. It was a fitting end to the 1920s, a decade as marked by greed and excess as the 1980s. The administration had been warned many times of the threat that high tariffs posed to the functioning of the world economy, but tariffs were, in the words of U.S. historian Robert S. McElvaine, "as American as apple pie, or at least as American as the Republican party."[12] High import levies were, as economist Joseph Schumpeter put it, "the household remedy" of the Grand Old Party.[13]

"The Hawley-Smoot Act, conceived in 1929, was the last will and testament of the New Era's 'every man for himself' ethic," McElvaine noted in his book *The Great Depression*. "It was motivated, as tariffs almost always are, by the greed of special interests. Fittingly, this relic of the prosperity decade left as a further legacy of the twenties a deepening of the Depression that other aspects of that era had already produced."[14]

Retaliation in the form of similar measures came swiftly from Europe, setting off a calamitous decline in trade, a nasty round of financial collapses, and a tidal wave of human misery. The volume of world trade fell by more than half between 1929 and 1932. The tariff-lowering Reciprocal Trade Act of 1934, promoted by Democratic President Franklin D. Roosevelt and his secretary of state, Cordell Hull, proved to be too little and too late. The liberal internationalism of Roosevelt and Hull, of course, bore not the least resemblance to P.I., and in fact contained the seeds of globalization in its current form. But it did mark a clear break with Republican isolationism, a force that nonetheless remained robust right up to its "Fortress America" policy outlook of the 1960s.

The responsibility does not lie all on one side — it never does in these matters. Many workers in 1930 were under the illusion that high tariffs would save their jobs, and the American Federation of Labor joined the National Association of Manufacturers in supporting the Hawley-Smoot Act. With their European competitors later pulverized by the war, U.S. industrialists eventually cottoned on to the fact that their interests lay in freer trade, and the Republican Party under Eisenhower and Nixon followed them to that conclusion (while still heeding their numerous pleas for countervailing duties and quotas in all manner of special circumstances). But the American right still has not exorcised itself of its protectionist demons. The Fortress America mentality shows up today in the likes of Pat Buchanan, that loathsome practitioner of the politics of exclusion, and the appalling Ross Perot, who was made a billionaire through lucrative public contracts and then complained that government was spending too much.

Those who hold liberal or leftist views have a choice. They can leave the torch of protectionism to the troglodytes and move on to something more promising. They can reclaim their internationalist heritage and work to redirect the course of globalization instead of moping about the way the current course is creating a sense of disempowerment. The political conjuncture of the 1980s made it possible for the corporate sector to set globalization on a track of its choosing. It is long past time for other sectors of society in Canada and elsewhere to work together and embolden their governments, not to abandon free trade, which is a necessary condition for the economic strength our quality of life depends upon, but to insist on higher standards in the way it is conducted and a more equitable sharing of its benefits.

The Global Village and the Potemkin Village

In the years after the Second World War there was a "global village." It is worth remembering that this notion, which emerged from the fertile brain of Canada's Marshall McLuhan, is essentially an American vision, and the heart of the village is American culture, American technology, American finance and American power. The post-Second World War scientific and technological revolution made modern concepts of globalism plausible; indeed, it made them appear as a seamless, natural, objective process. Describing giant corporations as "multinational" corporations on the basis that they operated throughout the world obscured the fact that most of them were American companies controlled by American owners that operated within the priorities of the American political system.

Actually, there were two villages: the American village and the Soviet Potemkin village. It was the second village that made the first one possible, even acceptable. Postwar American hegemony in the capitalist world and the Cold War with the Communist world were intricately related.

The Cold War came to America and Europe relatively effortlessly. The political repercussions were altogether beneficial to the established order in that they confined and subsequently nullified any political debate and certainly curbed the threatened rambunctious North American trade union movement. Consider, for example, the ability of the North American trade union movement not only to defend its wartime gains but to extend its power in 1945–46 in contrast with its currently manifest impotence, or the way the bipartisan Cold War policy weakened the British Labour Party and has made it irrelevant.

The Cold War also provided the political backdrop for maintaining the American economy on a permanent war footing. (We are reminded of the importance of having such a backdrop as the U.S. Defense Department struggles to find new rationales for maintaining its power and scope in the 1990s.) The long-term effects of the militarization of the economy are highly debatable. In the 1940s and 1950s, however, military spending — one of the chief forms Keynesian economics has taken in the United States — clearly played a role in preventing a postwar depression, keeping employment levels high, and funding the technological innovation that fuelled economic growth: what longtime business writer Peter Drucker calls the "productivity revolution."[15] Although military spending remained substantial after 1945, it did fall very sharply from wartime levels, and many economists predicted then that rapid demilitarization would indeed create a depression. With hindsight, economists later concluded that deferred consumption actually played the major role in fuelling the rapid growth that followed, as wartime savings went to work to relieve pent-up demand.

Drucker traces the development of the computer back to seventeenth-century mathematics but credits the enormous resources of the U.S. Defense Department with finally putting all the elements together (incidentally, after the immediate goal of the research — to track German fighter planes — had ceased to be relevant).[16] It has been estimated that in the 1950s and 1960s, nine of every ten major innovations had at least some connection to the military sector (although in more recent decades the links are less clear).[17] In this sense, the vast budget of the U.S. military has served the national economy of the United States. It is worth noting that the research facilities in which these technological advances originated were heavily subsidized, generally controlled and, at times, actually owned by the state.

American military power and American economic power went hand in hand. Prosperity in the United States was based on a number of factors, domestic and international: unprecedented levels of domestic consumption; foreign markets for U.S. goods, strengthened by U.S. aid under the Marshall Plan and other schemes and by the relative absence of competition from other industrial countries; technological advance; transfer of wealth to the United States by companies operating abroad; and the Keynesian policies, both military and civilian, of the U.S. government.

In this environment, all Americans, and especially the most militant mass industrial unions, were able to identify completely — socially, economically and politically — with the goals of the postwar American state. The global economy manifesting itself in postwar reconstruction — the American Century — created the state of all the people. Or at least so it seemed for a while. It was in this period that the myth of the "classless" society (in a country where industrialization had been accompanied by especially intense class conflicts) took hold most strongly. It is particularly interesting in this respect to reread some of John Kenneth Galbraith's early works on the nature of American capitalism and his theory of "countervailing power" in which the American trade union movement is considered to be part of the structure of the economic, political and social system.[18]

The willingness of the trade-union movements in America and Europe to associate themselves with the foreign and domestic policy of their postwar governments has often been commented on and documented — for example, the cheerful willingness to import the gangster Hal Banks and make him a Canadian trade unionist or the workings of the CIA within the AFL-CIO and affiliates such as the Newspaper Guild and the United Auto Workers. The term "labor statesman" was even coined, although it is not heard so often now. American journalist David Halberstam in *The Reckoning* deals at great length and detail about how the UAW in particular helped smash the legitimate leadership of the Japanese auto unions and replace it with a gangster element that created a passive and docile workforce in the plants. Remarkably, Halberstam does this without the least sense of irony.

It is unlikely that the United States would have achieved domestic social peace and international dominance so readily in the postwar period without an enemy to mount a Pax Americana against, and the ease with which the "Great Soviet Ally" became the focus of evil has long buttressed arguments that the Cold War was a carefully planned strategy. However, arguing the convenience and efficacy of the Cold War to the ruling establishments on both sides of the curtain does not mean accepting the premise that it was a preconceived strategy for the world, emerging from the ashes of the war. If one follows that line of reasoning faithfully, one is left to puzzle why Germany and Japan, in the long run the main beneficiaries of the Cold War, were not involved or even in a position to be consulted by the U.S. on its strategy, at least at the initial stages. Just because a policy turns out to be fortuitous does not mean that it was planned. Fortunately for humanity, the Law of Unintended Consequences sometimes creates positive consequences for the initiators.

America Faces East and West

As early as 1945 and 1946, even before Winston Churchill's famous speech at Fulton, Missouri, various American and European statesmen were considering the shape of postwar Europe. In early 1947, William C. Bullitt, a top U.S. State Department official, publicly proposed the creation of a European Federation of Democratic States to "face up to Russia."[19] The subsequent creation of the Marshall Plan was predicated on the concept of Europe as a single entity, which led directly to the European Community and greatly accelerated the pace of what we today call globalization. The push towards European union not only arose from the realization of the baneful fruit of disunion but also harkened back to the fundamental process that had begun a century earlier.

Describing Europe's postwar recovery, American historian Paul Kennedy develops the argument that economic progress in Europe was retarded and distorted by the attempts at national exclusivity as well as the wars and invasions that have ravished the continent.

Even before the fighting, Europe's "natural" economic development — that is, growth which evolved region by region, as new sources of energy and production revealed themselves, as new markets took off, as new technology spread — had been distorted by the actions of the nationalistically inclined *machtsaat*. . . . It was thus impossible to maximize Europe's economic growth. . . . Now after 1945, there were "new Europeans" like Monnet, Spaak and Hallstein determined to create economic structures which would avoid the mistakes of the past, but there was also a helpful and beneficent United States, willing (through the Marshall Plan and other aid schemes) to finance Europe's recovery provided it was done as a cooperative venture.[20]

Kennedy points out that American economic assistance, particularly in its procurement policies during and after the Korean War, not only created the conditions for the survival of Japanese industry but also led to its fantastic growth and development. And in some measure, largely through the operation of the Law of Unintended Consequences, the linking of military with economic considerations created a Pacific Rim economy, which is likely to become the dominant economic factor of the next century. In other words the "new" Europe arose out of the ashes of the war and the "new" Asia bypassed the national exclusivity described by Kennedy.

There has been a debate in the United States between the "Atlanticists" and the "Pacificists" about which way the country should face since it became a continental nation. While modern America has generally ignored President Washington's appeal to keep out of European affairs, its relationship with Europe has been of a completely different order from its concerns over the Pacific. Mythology has it that America has traditionally rejected a corrupt and degenerate Europe. Yet it has always seen itself as basically a European nation. Its institutions and culture are European. America always aped the mores and manners of the continent. (John Kenneth Galbraith once estimated that the flow of money from America in the form of dowries to titled but impecunious Europeans significantly altered the nation's balance of payments.) Even today, social commentators are apt to make the point that Americans follow, shall we say, the ups and downs of British Royals as much as the British themselves. It has often been noted that the Americans view royalty on much the same plane as movie stars, a lofty plane indeed.

America also looked to Europe for immigrants, the slave trade being the sole exception. Although America would from time to time accept temporary coolie labour, Asian immigration was discouraged, and when it was allowed a whole range of racist regulations, from the head tax to the prevention of family immigration, prevailed. Racism was deeply embedded in the body politic of both Canada and the U.S. and it cut across the board politically, from Mackenzie King worrying about racial purity to militant trade union leaders refusing to work with Asians "because they smell." It should also be remembered that Woodrow Wilson pointedly refused to include a condemnation of racism in the charter of the League of Nations, even after his erstwhile ally, Japan, specifically asked for such an inclusion.

Nevertheless, it was the Pacific that captured the imagination and the early imperialist strivings of the U.S. Just as in the days of the Monroe Doctrine, its rivals were mainly the British and the fading remnants of the older European empires. Even before Canada was given the right and freedom to operate in international affairs it engaged in a diplomatic favour for the United States by convincing the British to break their Pacific naval treaty with Japan in 1920. Canada did this by pointing out to the British that the Americans would consider the renewal of this alliance a hostile act. According to Paul Johnson, the refusal to extend the treaty helped to weaken the British position in the Pacific fatally.

Perhaps the Americans were not so much rivals to the Europeans as successors. As Franklin Roosevelt waged war against the Japanese empire and its Asian "Co-Prosperity Sphere," he was merely hurrying the succession along. There is no question about whom the Americans saw as their enemy and who was their ally: Japan was the enemy and poor China was the American protectorate. That this got turned on its ear is perhaps the most important outcome of the Cold War and one of the more revealing manifestations of the Law of Unintended Consequences. Thus if one can make a case that the Cold War supported and advanced American interests in Europe, in Asia from Korea through China into Vietnam it was an unmitigated American disaster. The recreation of Japan is the American imperial nightmare come true. Because the U.S. recreated its nemesis, the irony that it was all done to protect the "free world" from monolithic communism should not be lost.

With Asia, particularly Japan, paranoia goes to the wellsprings of the American imagination. Remember the cry of "who lost China?" Even though China was never owned, this slogan convulsed American politics for a generation, during which China replaced Japan as the home of the yellow peril. America's disastrous wars in Korea and Indochina were among this period's more memorable events.

But Japan was always America's strategic enemy. After the war, John Foster Dulles patronizingly suggested that Japan begin to rebuild its economy by concentrating on toys and novelties — "those pretty little paper umbrellas that decorate cocktail glasses." Dulles, and for that matter American policymakers in general, rarely if ever stopped at patronizing suggestions, and studies of early postwar policies in Japan certainly suggest that the Americans were quite willing to cripple the Japanese economy permanently. No thought was ever given to an Asian Marshall Plan. Other events intervened. The Cold War in Asia began two years after it started in Europe, and it quickly became a hot one.

The famous "domino theory" dates from the Korean War, a war that Dulles, who became Secretary of State in 1953, often characterized as not being about Korea but about Japan. This theory became the rationale for American policy in support of the French in Indochina and later for direct U.S. involvement in Vietnam. Although it was often portrayed as being about the spreading of the armed forces of Vietnam into surrounding countries, the real fear was the potential control by China of the vast natural resources of Asia at the expense of resource-poor Japan. Japan was the essential domino of the theory, and the effort to build, sustain and develop the Japanese economy and keep it onside in the Cold War was the heart and soul of American policy in the Pacific. As Dulles testified, "If Southeast Asia were lost, this would lead to a loss of Japan. The situation of the Japanese is hard enough with China being commie. You would not lose Japan immediately, but from there on out the Japs would be thinking of how to get on the other side."[21]

President Eisenhower was even more explicit: "If we don't assist Japan . . . Japan is going Communist. . . . Then instead of the Pacific being an American lake it is going to be a Communist lake. . . . Of course we don't want to ruin our own industries to keep Japan on our side, but we must give them assistance." The growth of the European and Japanese economies to the point where they would be seen as something like Frankenstein's monster by the U.S. was for the future. To contrast what was then and what is now in American policy, one needs only to repeat the oft-quoted testimony of U.S. trade representative Mickey Kantor: "The days when we could subordinate our economic interests to foreign policy or defense concerns are long past."[22]

At the time, however, the assertion of American power in the Pacific, the creation of the American lake, dictated a detour around Japan. The U.S. provided a military shield and encouraged the development and growth of Japanese industry and trade both directly and indirectly. (Toyota was about to declare bankruptcy when it received its first order for jeeps and military vehicles for the UN forces in Korea.)

The early literature on Japan, such as David Halberstam's *The Reckoning*, takes a rather bemused approach to Japanese growth and the implications of this growth for America. In a real sense it is a case of the imitator who learns the lessons better than the teacher, but the central point was that Japan was taught what to do and given the wherewithal to do it by the generous U.S. For all that, it is a rather benign message, for this was early in the game and there were markets enough for all. Indeed, both the American and Japanese automobile industries were booming along with joint ventures and production-sharing agreements. Nor did it really matter that Japan was moving into the consumer camera and electronics businesses: most of the patents were still held in America, and American industry was occupied with the more lucrative defence contracts. The Americans were providing not only the means and market for Japan's economic growth but also the defensive shield. Now would the Japanese be grateful and respectful enough?

In Europe, America provided the same shield and with the Marshall Plan certainly aided reconstruction — especially in its enemy, Germany. But the relationship with Europe was never one of teacher to pupil, and the screams of who lost us Poland or Bulgaria were muted if heard at all. The U.S. accepted its role as leader, claimed its rights as banker and financier of European recovery and became enormously wealthy in the process. But it never saw the Atlantic as an American lake and it accepted that organizations such as NATO not only expressed American power but limited that power as well.

But Asia is something else, something more serious and historically conditioned, in the experience and dreams of America. Manifest Destiny has included the notion of one great republic stretching from the Arctic Circle to the Rio Grande. It has included the Monroe Doctrine, which envisions American suzerainty of the Western Hemisphere. It has also included the concept of the Pacific as an American lake.

American naval strategist Admiral Alfred T. Mahan brilliantly advanced the doctrine of naval superiority in his major work *The Influence of Sea Power upon History*, which guided American strategy to the end of the Second World War. Theodore Roosevelt applied Mahan's theories first against the crumbling Spanish empire and later to ensure the permanent power of the navy through a complex system of bases from Hawaii to the Philippines to Guam. The aim of this military presence was to thwart the ambitions of Japan.

Control of the Pacific was the cornerstone of American policy during the Second World War as the United States formed alliances with nationalist leaders such as Ho Chi Minh in Vietnam, Sukarno in Indonesia, and even Mao Zedong in China — not only to strengthen the fight against Japan but also to ensure that France, Britain and Holland, the former colonial powers displaced by the Japanese, would not be able to return and compete with America in the Pacific. The Asia experts who questioned the Asian policy promoted by the hard-line ideologues — the infamous "China Lobby" — were not really "soft on Communism" in the way that they were portrayed. Rather, they saw American interests against both the old European colonialists and the Japanese colonialists as being advanced in some sort of alliance even with Communist-led nationalist movements. This argument haunts American politics to this day. But in any case, Manifest Destiny for the Americans was control of the Pacific, and with the partial exception of the Cold War period when the USSR allied with "Red China" seemed more menacing, Japan was the only power that was seen to stand in the way.

Private International Money

In time, the political, economic and technological conditions that made the postwar American-dominated global economy possible slowly eroded. The costs of maintaining world hegemony began to outweigh the benefits. The allies carefully nurtured by the United States became competitors. The global village began to divide into regional blocs. In the end, the "American century" lasted only twenty-five years. Its soft underbelly turned out to be the international financial system. Paradoxically, this was also the weak point in the prevailing idea of national sovereignty. Changes within the international financial system spelled the end of one global economy and paved the way for the new one that has not yet fully emerged.

American hegemony was the underlying assumption of the financial system set up in 1944 at Bretton Woods. The U.S. dollar was to be, in effect, the international medium of exchange. Dollars flowed out of the United States through World Bank and bilateral loans, through American foreign investment, and through U.S. military bases abroad. They flowed back in as payment for the American goods that dominated world markets. Dollars could also be redeemed for gold in the United States at a fixed rate of $35 an ounce. To maintain stability, countries were required to keep their currencies at a fixed exchange rate against the U.S. dollar. (One country was exempted from this requirement: because of the size and volatility of U.S. dollar flows in and out of Canada, it was allowed to float its dollar from 1950 on. As in many other fields, Canadian monetary vulnerability anticipated that of the rest of the world.)

This system stayed more or less in equilibrium through most of the 1950s. By the end of the decade, however, as European and Asian economies recovered, demand for American goods had begun to fall. It was no longer possible to repatriate all the dollars that left the United States, especially when the dollar outflow was intensified by the Vietnam War in the late 1960s. One result of this imbalance was a series of gold drains and balance-of-payments crises, in response to which the Kennedy and Johnson administrations took a series of corrective measures that had at best temporary effects. (Canada repeatedly sought exemption from these measures, hastening the development of an integrated North American financial market.) In 1971, when it had become clear that stopgap measures were no longer adequate, Richard Nixon ended the convertibility of the dollar into gold and sent the Bretton Woods system into terminal crisis.

Efforts to patch up the system after 1971 all failed, and floating exchange rates became the norm. Most Western European countries soon decided to float together rather than separately; in effect, other Western European currencies became pegged to the deutsche mark, which began to occupy a position within Europe that was not so different from the one the U.S. dollar had previously occupied internationally. The dollar, however, remained the chief medium of international exchange.

The international monetary instability of the 1960s also had another and in the long run even more significant effect. The U.S. dollars that remained outside the United States took on a life of their own. Banks and multinational corporations discovered that if these dollars were held outside the U.S. they could escape the regulatory efforts of the U.S. government. In fact, the growing quantity of these Eurodollars, as they came to be called, was one of the major contributing factors to the ineffectiveness of those efforts. A national currency is, in principle, an instrument of the government that issues it, which seeks to influence the national economy by regulating its availability and the conditions of its use. Eurodollars were subject to no such restrictions. They were the beginnings of a stateless currency, and they proved extremely useful to multinational banks and corporations. While international financial conditions have undergone a series of drastic changes since the 1960s, Eurocurrency markets (Eurodollars have been joined by other currencies set free of their national moorings) have survived and grown through all of them.

The precipitous increase in the price of oil in the 1970s put billions of U.S. dollars in the hands of OPEC governments, which deposited most of them in First World banks in the form of Eurodollars. Looking for places to lend this money, the banks found willing customers in Third World governments and asked few questions about how those governments operated or what was being done with the funds. By the early 1980s the results of this policy had matured into the Third World debt crisis, and the banks found other outlets for their Eurodollars. They went into the American deficit, mergers and acquisitions, megaprojects — indeed almost everywhere except the productive economy.[23]

At the same time, led by New York's Citibank, banks and investment houses in the United States and elsewhere placed increasing emphasis on expanding their international operations, selling securities in a variety of markets. Computer technology made it possible to transfer large sums of money instantaneously across national borders, further undermining traditional techniques of regulation such as exchange controls, which in any case had largely disappeared. While the original purpose of the exchange of currencies had been to finance international trade, by the 1980s a huge market in currencies had grown up that had nothing to do with trade. The average daily volume of activity on the world's foreign exchange markets in 1989 was estimated at US$640 billion, more than eighty times the volume of world trade.[24] Economist Bernard Élie describes the end result of these changes as the "marketization" of international finance.[25]

One example of the kind of deal fostered by these new circumstances is described by Roy C. Smith, himself an international banker with the New York-based firm Goldman Sachs, in his book *The Global Bankers.*[26] It seems that after Walt Disney opened its Tokyo Disneyland in the mid-1980s, it became concerned about having lots of yen with no hedge against future exchange-rate changes. The simple solution was to borrow long-term in yen, paying off the loan with their continuing yen income. A second suggestion was the Euroyen market, where Disney might be able to get a better deal.

> Another banker then approached the Disney team with a different idea. A major French government agency had recently borrowed yen in Japan in the domestic bond market. It had had to wait six months to do so, but when its number came up, rates were very attractive, and the issue was done very close to the Japanese government bond rate. "But the French don't really want the yen," explained the banker. "They think the yen/French franc rate will probably increase, making their yen debt more expensive to service. The French want to get rid of the yen. What they want are ECUs [European currency units]."

Disney accepted the banker's proposal, issuing Ecu bonds in the Euromarket and swapping the proceeds with the French agency for its yen.

But if the marketization of international finance opened up a variety of possibilities for multinational corporations and banks with global ambitions, it imposed new constraints on governments and especially on the institution that — more than a flag, perhaps even more than an airline (see chapter six) — had come to symbolize sovereignty in the twentieth century: the central bank.

To be sure, central bankers were still very powerful figures in their respective countries, perhaps more powerful than ever. After all, it was Federal Reserve Board chair Paul Volcker, not Jimmy Carter or Ronald Reagan, who took the lead in ratcheting up interest rates to 20 per cent at the beginning of the 1980s, contributing greatly to the length and depth of the 1982 recession. It was Bank of Canada governor John Crow, not Brian Mulroney, whose "zero-inflation policy" led to high interest rates and a high Canadian dollar starting at the end of the 1980s, exacerbating the negative effects of the Free Trade Agreement and wiping out much of the gain it might have brought. And German economic hegemony in Europe has been exercised more by Bundesbank presidents Karl Otto Pöhl and Helmut Schlesinger than by Chancellor Helmut Kohl.[27]

But central bankers' power has been increasingly subject to the approval of the high rollers in the international currency markets. This was demonstrated in 1990 when the Bank of Canada tried to reduce interest rates; the ensuing precipitous drop in the Canadian dollar forced the bank to reverse its course. It was demonstrated even more strikingly in the autumn of 1992 when currency traders put severe downward pressure on whatever happened to be the currency of the week: now the British pound, now the Italian lira, now the Canadian dollar. Britain and Italy were driven out of Europe's Exchange Rate Mechanism, Spain was forced to devalue its peseta, and the cause of European monetary union, to which the EC countries had agreed a year earlier at Maastricht, suffered a severe setback. Finally, in another currency crisis in the summer of 1993, the Exchange Rate Mechanism was more or less definitively derailed.

For central bankers, and for that matter governments, to exercise effective power in this context, they would have to do it collectively. (Thus, concerted action by the Bundesbank and the Banque de France prevented a devaluation of the franc in the fall of 1992. France calls its efforts to keep the franc at its existing exchange rate against the deutsche mark its *franc fort* policy; ironically, *Francfort*, or Frankfurt, is where the Bundesbank has its headquarters.)

Central bankers do meet regularly, most notably in get-togethers eight times a year in the offices of the Bank for International Settlements in Basel, Switzerland. They are often more responsive to one another than to the politicians who appointed them, and at least since the 1970s they have been largely united in their insistence on giving primacy to keeping inflation down and refusing to be distracted by annoying side-issues such as unemployment. But they do not regulate the international economy, and to the extent that they might be capable of any such achievement it would only be at the expense of their already tenuous accountability to political authorities in their home countries.

The emergence of a privatized international financial system has effects well beyond the financial sphere. One reason why people were increasingly receptive to the arguments of politicians such as Ronald Reagan and Margaret Thatcher in the late 1970s and early 1980s was that the economic effectiveness of governments was in fact diminishing. American economist Howard Wachtel has observed:

As supranationalism weakens the government's ability to manage its economy, the argument that government should step aside and turn over all responsibility to private markets seems more valid. This is precisely what happened in the decade after the end of Bretton Woods. Governments abdicated their public responsibility over international money, and this produced a largely unmanageable world economy, where private actors played the lead roles and governments had the bit parts. The supranational process erodes the public's role in economics and creates the very self-fulfilling prophecy that permits a free-market ideology to gain currency.[28]

Add in government debts and deficits, whose origins are complex but not unrelated to the chronic financial instability that began in the 1960s,[29] and all the elements are in place for the idea that government is part of the problem rather than part of the solution to become increasingly credible, as indeed it did during the 1980s. The most obvious emblems of this idea are the decade-long reigns of Reagan and Bush in the United States, Thatcher in Britain and Mulroney in Canada. Perhaps even more striking, however, has been the phenomenon of the social democratic government of the right, as seen in various parts of the world in the 1980s and 1990s. Whatever their initial intentions, Labour governments in Australia and New Zealand, Socialist governments in France and Spain and NDP governments in several Canadian provinces ended up carrying out policies that were little different from those of governments that were right-wing as a matter of stated principle.

The emergence of a private international economy, complete with private international money, made it impossible to pretend that governments could exercise their functions in the same way as in the past. On the other hand, the social and economic effects of the idea that government's proper role was simply to fade into the background were all too clear by the early 1990s, and they contributed to the fall of Margaret Thatcher, the defeat of George Bush and the terminal unpopularity of Brian Mulroney.

Terrible Simplifiers

In the theory of the new global economy, the flow of capital investments from capital-rich areas to areas of rich economic potential develops and thus enriches the target area. What was once denounced as imperialist-colonialist exploitation is now eagerly sought. The only audience a Canadian finance minister addresses is the bond markets and the rating services. The same goes for a provincial finance minister, even one who happens to belong to the NDP. It now appears that the only thing socialism lacked was capital.

Again in theory, the flow of capital creates a national or local economy wherever it lands. The repatriation of dividends and interest payments enriches the capital-exporting country even more than the recipient. If good money is to be made in manufacturing computers, even more is to be made in the countries where the computers are used.

The success of this global model assumes at least two constants.

In the first place, there must be a demand for capital. This, however, can be assured only in the environment of an economic boom. As the world entered the 1990s, there was no boom, and there was plenty of capital chasing too few opportunities. With all the hokum in the press and among government economists, there was no problem in borrowing money — the problem was in paying it back. A booming economy can repay its debts; a declining one only gets into deeper debt because of the miracle of compound interest. And no cutbacks in expenditures can help because the nature of a modern government's expenditures go towards increasing economic activity and retrenchment is therefore counterproductive.

This latter point speaks to the second constant of a modern economy: the increasing complexity and scope of government activity. Governments now must do far more than borrow money to raise an army to fight a war. Over the twentieth century, they have assumed an increasing burden of activity in areas where the private sector has withdrawn or traditionally refused to participate: large parts of the transportation and communication infrastructure, education, social welfare. The wealth that accrues to the modern industrial or "postindustrial" state through taxes, borrowings and direct investments is spread about — unequally, but nevertheless in such a manner as to give the mass of people a stake in the national economy and thereby in the state.

This is a gradual process, but even before Karl Marx died in 1883 the idea that the working class, now crowded into the slums of the new industrial cities, had "nothing to lose but their chains" was seen as wildly exaggerated. The idea that the state was of little economic importance was a reflection of early-nineteenth-century capitalism. Engels's view of the state as only "armed men and prisons," constituting little more than the coercive powers of the ruling class, perhaps helps explain why that element of the state apparatus was the only one successfully managed by Communist revolutionaries when they assumed power. But it does not reflect the socioeconomic reality of the societies they sought to lead.

Economists such as John Kenneth Galbraith have noted that the essential problem with Marx lay in the contradiction between, on the one hand, practical involvement in building a grassroots movement and creating a minimum program of reforms and social gains and, on the other, the maximum program of overthrowing the very system the minimum program is trying to reform.[30] (The immediate goals of the *Communist Manifesto* were the forty-hour week, free education and the extension of the vote — hardly revolutionary now or even then.) The more people could strive for and achieve the gains of the minimum program, the more they would lose interest in the maximum program. Moreover, even in Marx's day, the fundamental Marxist assertion of the inability of the capitalist system to grow beyond a certain level and the certainty of its collapse seemed to be refuted by the growth of the global economy.

Both in Marx's time and today, the question has been whether the system can be reformed and thus become permanent or whether through its reform it will change into something else. Even after the collapse of the Communist system in Europe, the search for what it might change into continues. Peter Drucker suggests that we are heading for "post-capitalist society."[31] American economist Robert Heilbroner argues that the traditional ethos of capitalism — self-interest — must give way to some sort of social participation to cope with the malfunctions of the system "which require a transnational political counterforce."[32] The "integrating principle" of this counterforce is

> *participation* — the engagement of all citizens in the mutual determination of every phase of their economic lives through discussion and voting. . . . It assumes that social and economic equality has replaced social and economic inequality as the widely endorsed norm of the society, because equality seems best suited to enable individuals to lead the most rewarding lives they can.

Thus we have come back almost full circle to something not too far from Marx's vision of "from each according to his ability, to each according to his needs." This is interesting in itself, but the most intriguing circumstance is the time frame.

Marx used the phrase (whether he thought it up himself or borrowed it from someone else is a matter of historical debate) as part of his criticism of a new political program born of the merger of two working-class parties in Germany. The year was 1875. The Paris Commune had been crushed. A united Germany was growing in economic power, Bismarck was experimenting in early and primitive social legislation, and the German Social Democratic party was seeking ways to develop these reforms further just as it was naturally identifying itself with the state. Germans (including Social Democrats) were beginning to see, just as were other Europeans, that the growth, power and wealth of the state could protect and enrich everybody within its territory.

A generation later, as revolutionaries debated the workers' response to the coming war, it was relatively easy to prove that the bonds of solidarity were of class, not of nationality. But the nature of the state, the nation and nationality was undergoing a profound change that was far more difficult to assess. Lenin could, and did, toss these notions of the state aside as a temporary capacity to buy off either a "labour aristocracy" or even virtually a whole class. If this capacity was temporary, however, it was temporary for a long time. It has been buttressed by the relationship between the highly industrialized countries and the underdeveloped world, now yoked together in one global system. Massive amounts of money flow from South to North, allowing the favoured few (or relatively few) to discuss with confidence something called "people's capitalism."

Nineteenth-century philosophers like Marx and Hegel have been called "terrible simplifiers." Lenin, it would seem, can be added to this group, for he and his revolution are very much part of the nineteenth century in conceptual terms. Nowhere is this more obvious than in the oversimplification of national consciousness. And this national consciousness is very much related not only to the global economics of which Lenin wrote but also to the identification of the mass of the citizens with the state and its goals and ambitions.

We have described the period after the Second World War as the heyday of this identification, at least in the United States. *The Economist* writes about the "wonderful 1950s [when] . . . the term 'working-class' was banished from polite American discourse . . . as if even to breathe the phrase was to commit a crime against the achievements of the postwar years."[33] That, of course, was then. For a vision of the future *The Economist* quotes Charles Murray, a leading conservative social theorist:

> The number of the rich will grow more rapidly in the coming years. . . . Real wages for low skilled jobs will increase more slowly, if at all. . . . I fear the potential of producing something like a caste society, with the implication of utter social separation. . . . All the forces that I can discern will push American conservatism toward the Latin American model. . . . The Left have been complaining for years that the rich have too much power. They ain't seen nothing yet.

When the ruling class embarks on a program such as the one hinted at by Murray, and when the state is or at least claims to be powerless to stop it, the identification of ordinary citizens with the nation-state is bound to weaken (see chapter seven). "People's capitalism" works only in relative isolation and in an expanding economy. In Ontario, for example, its shelf life is currently limited as people try to adjust to working in the competitive atmosphere proclaimed with Mexico. The operative phrase now is "ratcheting down." Some employers have used the threat of moving operations to Mexico to get workers to agree to wage concessions. If this strategy succeeds on a large scale, it can lead to several possible consequences. If prices fell to the same extent as average wages, then wage-earners would not be substantially worse off. But if the owners of capital fattened their profit margins instead, then living standards in the North would suffer and the popular support the capitalist system now enjoys would be undermined.

And who will maintain the schools, the hospitals, the cultural institutions? Who will establish the political agenda or partially redistribute the wealth? The answer that all Western governments are giving is nobody at all. Thus, in Bob Rae's Ontario, where the dismantling of Ontario Hydro is under serious consideration, the words of the old Tory who created it, Sir Adam Beck, have an odd ring:

> I do not understand that any revelation has ever been made from Heaven to the effect that a democratic government commits an unpardonable sin when it assists in the establishment of a great and necessary public work for the well-being of the people of whose interests it is the trustee.[34]

All this, we are told, is passé in the new global economy in which the nation-state is rendered irrelevant. The idea of the government as the trustee of public interest, or even that there is a public interest, is scarcely heard. Drawn to its logical conclusion, the neoconservative program of weakening the state to recreate a truly unfettered economic environment brings us back to some new form of social Darwinism, which currently goes by the name of the "race to the bottom" and is the hidden agenda of some supporters of treaties such as NAFTA. The ascendancy of this program should remind us that not all the "terrible simplifiers" are on one side.

But if the continuing — and perhaps even increasing — need for some kind of authority representing and acting in the public interest is clear, difficult questions about the form this authority should take remain. Are existing national entities still effective units for exercising economic policy if corporations have transcended them? If technological change is undermining bureaucratic modes of organization, can the state find a better way of organizing itself? Will the relatively minimal and traditional forms of intervention embarked on in the United States by the Clinton administration merely open the way for more radical measures no one has yet contemplated? And if corporate globalization is to be effectively opposed, will citizens have to take sovereignty into their own hands? We look at these and other questions surrounding the nature of modern sovereignty in the next chapter.

Chapter 3

Globalization versus the Nation-State

Sovereignty and Association

When the late René Lévesque broke with the Quebec Liberal Party in 1967 to fight for Quebec independence, he formed a new political grouping which he called the *Mouvement Souveraineté-Association* — the sovereignty-association movement. This soon formed the nucleus of the Parti Québécois which, under Lévesque's guidance, espoused the vision of a sovereign Quebec in economic association with the rest of Canada.

Sovereignty-association failed to win majority support in a 1980 referendum, and years later the PQ altered its vocabulary to advance the less ambiguous notion of independence. Sovereignty-association was an unwieldy mouthful; looking back, it may seem now like a quaint concept that sprang at a particular moment from Quebec's fertile political soil. Lévesque never intended it as a universal theory. But in a strange way it defines the continuing evolution of relations between states on a global level. It takes account of the fundamental fact that people want control over their own affairs (sovereignty), but often tend at the same time to crave the security and the strength that larger units can provide (association). Among the many questions the world faces are what form these units should take and whether the traditional nation-state should remain the prime focus of political and economic organization.

An obvious starting point is the recognition that not even big countries, let alone small ones, can stand entirely on their own. Apart from Albania's former perpetual leader, Enver Hoxha, few twentieth-century thinkers have argued seriously that trade and investment ought ideally to be contained within national borders. The twin concepts of autarchy (absolute sovereignty) and autarky (absolute self-sufficiency) have not had an easy ride these last few decades, and Hoxha was the sort of ruler who gave both a bad name. His fiercely antirevisionist brand of communism may have made him a hero among Maoists, and his stern rejection of foreign political and economic contamination may have caused no lasting harm outside Albania's hermetic boundaries, but what he bequeathed to Albanians was the most seriously ravaged economy in Eastern Europe.

The nation-state is an inexact and, in some respects, an unfortunate creation. It does not always make sense as the prime focus of sovereignty, and countless wars have been fought in its name. Only in a few rare instances do the political boundaries of the state correspond to the reality of a nation comprising a single people sharing characteristics of language, culture and common origins. Nor are boundaries all-encompassing. The Hungarian nation spills into western Romania, and the Romanian nation spills into Moldova (the former Soviet republic of Moldavia). Serbian minorities in the former Yugoslav republics of Croatia and Bosnia-Herzegovina have made their presence felt all too bloodily. Outside Europe the situation is just as fraught with potential peril. Most African countries are veritable patchwork quilts of different ethnic groups.

In every nation-state the central authorities have striven, to a greater or lesser extent and with a greater or lesser use of coercion, to impose a common identity and a national sense of community. This presents a challenge in countries such as Canada where more than one set of national characteristics is recognized officially. It presents a different type of challenge in the numerous countries where minority cultures are suppressed by means we might not always condone. Some heterogeneous countries, most notably the United States, have done rather well at creating a strong national identity, although even there some strains are showing (see chapter seven). Others, such as Canada, have had a harder time of it. One of the stronger unifying characteristics among Canadians is simply that they prefer not to be Americans.

Some countries have responded to regional or ethnic differences by establishing federal systems of government that divide responsibilities between the central authorities and the provincial, state or cantonal level; each level of government is sovereign in certain areas of jurisdiction, although often there are overlaps and confusion. Other countries, particularly in Western Europe, have begun to devolve some powers to regional bodies in places such as Scotland and Catalonia.

But even where a particular nation-state has a homogeneous population (as in Japan or Sweden) or where it has managed to forge a strong sense of common purpose (as in the United States) — in other words, even in those countries where the legitimacy and coherence of the central government is not burdened by questions of language, ethnicity or regionalism — sovereignty is not absolute, and there are sound reasons why it should not be. People living in different countries have too many common interests in areas ranging from trade to the environment to human rights for all decision-making to be contained within national boundaries.

One of the more visible results of the exercise of national sovereignty has been the worldwide proliferation of customs posts, whose primary purpose is to restrict the flow of goods. The very existence of customs posts is an admission of failure, for it suggests that local producers cannot stand up to foreign competition or that local consumers cannot be trusted with whatever it is that may come in. It also assumes that national borders form the most logical trade boundaries.

For decades the world has been groping with a fundamental question: Is there really any compelling reason why goods should flow any less freely between sovereign states than within them? In a North American context, the question becomes whether goods should flow less freely from Michigan to Ontario than from Ontario to Manitoba or, to carry it a step further, whether Nova Scotia steelworkers who lose their jobs because of competition from Ontario should feel any happier than Ontario steelworkers who lose their jobs because of competition from Texas. Reasons of history have determined that Manitoba, Ontario and Nova Scotia all form part of the same sovereign country. Will a freer international flow of goods really erase this history and the shared values that might have arisen from it?

Again, sovereignty is not absolute, and we need not wallow in jargon about interdependence to emphasize this. Every time an international agreement or treaty is signed, its signatories give up a small piece of their sovereignty. Under the United Nations system, which since its inception has played an important part in defining relations between states, every sovereign state, no matter how tiny and insignificant, is the equal of every other sovereign state. This, of course, is a fiction and not even a polite fiction at that. If a country is big enough and powerful enough, it can violate its obligations under the United Nations charter and get away with it. The government of the sovereign Republic of Nicaragua has never acted to subvert the authority of the sovereign government of the United

States, but the inverse has been known to happen. In real life, some countries are more sovereign than others.

Still, even the United States government does tend, most of the time, to abide by most of the thousands of treaties to which it is a signatory, however inconvenient it sometimes finds this. It does so because it expects to receive some benefit in exchange for what amounts to yielding bits of its sovereignty. For example, it allows aircraft flown by British airline companies to land at U.S. airports because in return it gets landing rights for American companies at British airports. The U.S. side has grumbled that it hasn't got all it wants from this bilateral accord, but if it flexed its full sovereign muscle and barred British aircraft from landing in the U.S. there might be no direct air service at all between the two countries. (Lately the U.S. has even been respecting its bilateral air agreement with Nicaragua.) And however egregiously the U.S. may have breached the letter or the spirit of its trade agreement with Canada in certain instances, it has grudgingly acceded to rulings of a special bilateral panel; to do otherwise would be to harm the long-term interests of U.S. consumers and U.S. exporters for the short-term benefit of a handful of complainers.

Without some yielding of national sovereignty there can be little international commerce. Even Hoxha's Albania conducted some limited foreign trade. No country on earth, big or small, can pretend to be totally self-sufficient. Countries entering the General Agreement on Tariffs and Trade do so knowing it limits their sovereignty but bolsters their exports, as long as others play by the rules. And if sovereignty remained fully intact there could be few effective international controls in areas as diverse as contagious disease or toxic wastes or migratory birds or the ozone layer in the upper atmosphere, areas where national action alone would be ineffective. Many countries have agreed, for instance, to limit their sovereign right to emit ozone-destroying chemicals because they don't want their citizens to be fried by dangerous solar rays.

Since the time of Jean-Jacques Rousseau, there has been broad acceptance of the notion that the people are sovereign and governments exercise sovereignty in their name. This concept underpinned the constitution of the United States, and it influenced the great nineteenth-century socialist thinkers. Sad to say, governments of all political stripes often seem more prone to abuse the trust of the people than to respect it, but in democratic societies the people at least have a voice in choosing their rulers.

What happens, though, when sovereignty is handed over to someone else? We mentioned that national sovereignty may sometimes be shared with lower levels of government in a federal distribution of powers, and if this means that authority in appropriate areas is exercised closer to the people, then so much the better. But sovereignty can be distributed outward as well as inward. National governments may willingly relinquish some small bits of authority to the World Health Organization, or to the International Atomic Energy Agency, or to countless others among the bounteous alphabet soup of do-gooder world bodies attempting to perform tasks that national governments cannot manage on their own. Some do their jobs well and others are abysmal, but they are under the nominal if indirect control of the sovereign governments that banded together to create them.

Or national governments may agree to pool portions of their sovereignty in useful creations such as the European Community. The main task of the EC has been to break down trade barriers among its member states, but it has branched into other areas and given Western Europe a degree of economic and political coherence it might otherwise lack. Not all members — and especially not the British — have agreed on how much sovereignty should be ceded to Community headquarters in Brussels or to the European Parliament, but all agree that certain responsibilities can be met more effectively in Community hands than at the national level. Each member state still maintains a broad panoply of powers (sovereignty) while deriving benefits from being part of a larger bloc (association). Nascent trade groupings such as NAFTA in other parts of the world may steer away from formal EC-style structures, but member countries will still yield sovereignty in trade-related matters to benefit from association.

Or national governments may watch as sovereignty trickles away to a small coterie of financial and industrial giants. This trend is more ominous. The growing ability of big multinational companies to transfer huge amounts of capital at the push of a button or to move production facilities around the globe like pieces on a chess board enables them largely to escape the sovereign control of individual countries. Such corporations may be talented at minimizing costs and making efficient use of resources, and this can be of general benefit to humanity — at least to the extent that a rising tide raises all boats. But if you don't have a boat, you could be in danger of drowning.

Multinational corporations are easy to demonize. We remember how in the early 1970s the giant ITT conglomerate looked set to devour the world, and then it was Exxon, and then it was someone else. Each had its comeuppance, and some of the more exaggerated fears back then proved unfounded. Turning the logic and conventional wisdom of the 1970s and 1980s on its ear, IBM, for example, was brought to its knees not by an even larger entity with even better economies of scale or by a conglomerate that found an even cheaper labour paradise but by upstart American firms such as Dell and Microsoft. The fate of IBM, and in another sense General Motors, is in part a reflection of bad management, poor corporate guesswork and shortsighted business goals as well as the communications and technological revolution. But the real problem is the reduction in the growth of the world economy, which has brought the industrialized countries to the brink of a depression. In this climate, yesterday's dynamos have become dinosaurs and the growth of most multinational corporations has been stifled.

In early 1993, *The Economist* published a survey of multinationals, the burden of which was that while multinationals were a significant aspect of the tangled skein of world economics, they have not grown as predicted; their numbers, far from being concentrated and reduced, have grown considerably; and they continue to look and act like corporate citizens of the countries of their birth.[1] Indeed, the bulk of their activities are at home or in adjacent regions. In short, the multinational has not developed in practice as it should have in theory. The theory of the market should play itself out until there is only one player, just as any game of Monopoly. But it never seems to happen. As *The Economist* points out, to travel in a certain direction does not mean to arrive.

Some of today's fears about the power of multinationals may also turn out to be exaggerated, and of course we keep hearing the usual arguments about how economic power is better left with bottom-line watchers than with out-of-touch civil servants and profligate politicians. But without imputing malicious intent to the big multinationals (even where it is deserved), and without wanting to place unnecessary obstacles in the way of economic efficiency, one has reason to be wary of their power. Government controls over industry and finance do have their drawbacks, but — and it is a big but — governments in most industrialized countries have to answer to their citizens in periodic consultations. They make at least a pretence of democratic practice.

Corporate democracy, on the other hand, is the quintessential oxymoron. Apart from the occasional consumer boycott, there are few ways of subjecting corporations to the popular will. Under most circumstances not even shareholders, with the exception of some very large ones, have much say. Only a small band of managers and directors exert direct influence, and as long as their decisions cause few disasters they need answer to nobody but themselves. Their investment decisions can make or break whole communities and entire regions, across the street or around the globe. Governments and workers know this and are having to tailor tax rates and wage demands accordingly. It's not getting easier to make corporations pay their share of the tax burden or to take responsibility for the welfare of those who serve them. In Canada, corporate income tax as a share of government revenues has dwindled steadily over the last three decades. To those who would argue that taxes on corporate profit hinder economic growth and job creation, we might point out that corporate taxes accounted for a more sizeable portion of Canadian tax revenues in the 1950s and 1960s, hardly the most sluggish period in the country's economic history. For instance, in the mid-1950s, roughly half of federal income tax revenues came from individuals and half from businesses. By the late 1980s, individuals' share had risen to nearly 80 per cent. In the 1961–62 fiscal year, corporate income tax accounted for 20.1 per cent of total federal revenues. In a steady slide, this fell to 11.0 per cent by 1988–89, in part because of a decline in corporate profits as a share of gross domestic product, but also in part because of lower tax rates — 18.8 per cent in 1988–89 compared to 31.0 per cent in 1961–62.

We have argued up to now that the nation-state is not always the most sensible place to focus sovereignty. Certain responsibilities can be handled better at the local or international levels, and there is reason to welcome some of the shifts that have been occurring away from national governments towards regional bodies on the one hand and supranational bodies such as the EC on the other. In an article entitled "The Nation-State on Trial," *Economist* Asian correspondent Jim Roher concluded:

For about 200 years the political instrument for trying to harness the divergent currents of economy and society has been the nation-state. If this sounds awfully recent, that is because it is. Germany and Italy did not exist as the world now knows them until just over a century ago. For thousands of years empires such as those of China and Rome and city-states such as Venice and Lubeck were the political units that counted. With the strains being increasingly put on the nation-state by both the race to a single global economy and by the enduring strength of local attachments, might not a world of city-states become attractive again?[2]

We think Roher is overstating the changes that have actually taken place. The race may be longer than anyone anticipates and the outcome quite uncertain. The enduring "local attachments" may find new and unanticipated expressions and the new economy may reflect the only immutable law of politics, the Law of Unintended Consequences. In the meantime, the global recession and the return of the Democrats to power in the United States have given that most unfashionable of institutions, the national government, a new lease on life.

Then, Now and Not Yet

The development of the global economy is often projected as a natural process that operates oblivious to — even mockingly towards — human intervention. Governments, even the most powerful, have no power against the movement of capital and the trade winds that blow.

However, serious economists and social critics ascribe ever greater powers to the governments of modern states as the world shrinks into one economy. While the whole concept of "globalism" includes notions of the decline, reduction and even elimination of the role and power of government, almost all suggestions of dealing with and adapting to the "new global economy" deal with direct government action on the economy. Indeed, the notion of the passive uninvolved government was never a realistic option or practice. Even leaving aside the massive intervention in the American economy by the state under Ronald Reagan in the name of the defence buildup, we are still left with the fact that Reagan handed more import relief to American companies than any other president in history.[3] And the Mulroney government, for all its cutbacks in social programs and services, never saw an industrial boondoggle or megaproject it didn't like.

In *The End of Laissez-Faire*, Robert Kuttner argues that the spirit of John Maynard Keynes is very much alive in the industrialized world. He notes that the United States was never able to convince the world of its so-called free-market system, even when it was the dominant economic power. Reaganism and Thatcherism divorced theory from practice even during their heyday. Now, according to

Kuttner, "after a detour of nearly fifty years, we have cycled back to the agenda of 1944 [the Bretton Woods agreement]: pluralism, peace and planning."[4] This may be wishful thinking, but it does indicate that the power of government or public authority has not been totally marginalized.

According to the noted American historian Arthur Schlesinger, "The cherished national myth ascribes the economic development of the United States to the operation of unfettered individual enterprise, as if the mighty economy of the twentieth century had sprung by immaculate conception from the loins of Adam Smith."[5] Schlesinger moves from that opening statement to a systematic refutation of the central myth of American economic history — America as the great laboratory of Adam Smith.

He goes on to detail the tradition of state involvement in American economic growth, especially in such fields as infrastructure and education. Interestingly, among the initiatives he cites in the pre-Civil War period is a tariff policy and industrial protection that were almost exactly the same as John A. Macdonald's in Canada. Indeed, if you add the American National Policy of the early nineteenth century to the prescriptions of President Clinton's budget director, Alice Rivlin, for decentralization and a form of cooperative federalism to advance economic reconstruction, then one can visualize the new superstate on the North American continent resembling the Canada of the mid-1970s more than the U.S. of the 1990s.

Schlesinger's essay fits well into his thesis of the cycles of American history and especially into the largest body of his work which deals with the coming and going of the New Deal. As he elaborates on the waxing and waning of "activist governments," he develops the conditions that bring forward state interventionist theories and policies — remarkably like the conditions prevailing today. Schlesinger thus anticipates the coming of Bill Clinton (the essay was published in 1986). What he doesn't anticipate is the sudden demise of the Cold War, which was the condition of state intervention in all aspects, but especially the economic aspect, of society. There has never been any talk of the ugly brutish hand of the socialistic state in the communities and industries that depend on defence spending. Clinton's task is made much easier as he assumes the traditional function of the state in industries that must now make the transition to civil purposes.

If there once was a headlong rush into the borderless, stateless global economy, then the election of Bill Clinton has at the very least slowed that process down. If the U.S. won't play, there won't be a game. Indeed, the whole thrust of the Clinton administration, intellectually driven by people such as Robert Reich and Hillary Rodham Clinton, speaks to the power of a national government, speaking and acting in defence of its own perceived interests. It does not represent a global authority speaking and acting in the interests of the world community. Nor for that matter is it acting in defence of the trading bloc it aspires to organize and control. Moreover, it is exercising a power that other lesser states and governments do not have.

In the context of the jaded politics of the times, the tendency will be to underestimate the change that Clinton actually represents. The issues that have been opened up — medicare and the whole social security system, training and education, and above all the linkage of employment, welfare and urban decay — call for action far beyond that contemplated, much less proposed, by the administration. A proper analogy, we believe, is to the early days of the Roosevelt administration, as that president came to grips with the depth of the problems and quickly realized that the proposed solutions (a balanced budget, for one) were ineffectual and even meaningless. An original intention to be merely open to change was galvanized into becoming an agent of change.

In a boom, it is fashionable to believe that the economy can operate on automatic pilot. It is not possible even to think this way in a slump. Therefore the difference between then and now is a crucial one. *Then* was when the economies of the Western world were booming, capital was bubbling out of the cornucopia and for a relatively brief moment in economic history the theoreticians of "supply side" held sway. In these conditions, the nation-state, when it was no longer needed to organize the Cold War, could also be seen as no longer needed to organize the market, or even provide such services as roads, bridges and schools — the things that the market needed but was reluctant to pay for and that were therefore traditionally financed by the state.

In France, and particularly Germany with its postwar corporatism, the rhetoric never really matched the reality. Even the rhetoric was dispensed with in Japan. Efforts on both continents were internally coordinated to link the national economies with technology. For example, European (and now Asian) efforts to claim a place in the consumer aircraft field, ridiculed by the Americans during the Caravelle and Concorde era and ignored as Airbus began development, are now a cause of panic. During the days when the American market was personified by Ivan Boesky and Michael Milken and the defence budget looked after a large part of Boeing's needs, there was no problem. Now there is, and the first thing dispensed with is talk of interdependence within the global village. Also made quaint is the talk about the impotence of government and good fairy of free-market competition floating across borders, oceans and continents touching winners with her magic wand and giving a knee to the groin of the losers.

Now equally clearly means the Japanese economic freefall, the new European recession and the economic chaos in Eastern Europe. For example, the collapse of the Japanese real estate market has acted as a massive sponge on the world's capital market, compounding the economic black hole of Eastern Europe. Japan, which was exporting more than $100 billion yearly in the mid-1980s, is now bringing it back. In 1991 it returned some $36 billion over foreign investments.[6] Analysts commenting on this reversal of capital flow say it was relatively unnoticed because of the American recession and the declining need for investment capital. However, if the American recession is over, the Japanese one is not and the European one seems just about to begin.

In this connection the Clinton 1993 stimulus package is important not so much for its hesitant and limited character or its failure to get past the Republican opposition in Congress but as a demonstration of the American government's new willingness to create investment capital and enter the market directly. There are American economists who are willing to argue that John Maynard Keynes never died but has been hiding in the Pentagon lo these many years. Some add that Ronald Reagan was a closet Keynesian with his tax cuts and military spending that served to stimulate the economy. Be that as it may, the point is that Keynes seems to be coming out of hiding and is poised to stride the halls of the American government as in the old days of the New Deal.

Now is also clearly the time for the reassertion of the nation-state, which is the essence of Clinton's appeal to the United States. Manchester *Guardian* correspondent Martin Woollacott, for example, cites Clinton for embarking on "a program which is, above all else, one of national renewal [with his] appeal to patriotism."[7] With all the facile talk about the limitations of sovereignty implicit in the new globalism, it should be borne in mind that the leading powers — the United States, Japan and Germany — still have a great deal of sovereignty at their command. The loss was primarily for the weaker powers, the junior partners. There is no economic treaty between nations constructed between such unequal partners as that between the United States and Canada.[8] Countries in the European Community are of vastly different sizes, but not even Germany is dominant to anywhere near the extent that the U.S. is in North America. The Canadian economy is less than a tenth of the American, and in the FTA Canada gave up much of the residual control of its economy and now depends on the good offices and intentions of its "partner." And even more control could be lost if the subsidies code foreseen in the treaty is ever negotiated.

The neoconservative monetary and fiscal policies of the government have wreaked more havoc on Canada than any trade agreement, but the FTA has made it more difficult to repair the damage done. The U.S. relinquished little sovereignty in the FTA, and it seemed able to reconstruct its economy after the débâcle — something Canada seemed incapable of doing for some time afterward, for a variety of reasons extending well beyond the FTA. Thus Canada appeared paralysed, waiting for the rising tide of recovery to flow north. With all the pros and cons of the arguments circulating about the FTA, the loss of sovereignty is indisputable. Canadians could not even determine whether they would be part of NAFTA, as they would be governed by it in any case. Under those circumstances they could only sit on the sidelines and wonder what would happen and whether it would all work out.

The continuing role and power of the state has also encouraged what has been described as the "relationship enterprise." *The Economist* describes the relationship enterprise as a group of powerful corporations coming together to develop a given project. It quotes an American management consultant's paper at the annual meeting of the World Economic Forum entitled "The Global Corporation — Obsolete So Soon":

> Boeing, British Airways, Siemens, TNT (an Australian parcel delivery firm) and SNECMA (a French aero-engine maker) might together win a deal to build ten new airports in China. As part of this, British Airways and TNT would receive preferential and landing slots, the Chinese government would buy all state aircraft from Boeing-SNECMA and Siemens would provide the air-traffic control systems of all ten airports.[9]

There is a whole literature on various multinational corporations, particularly in automobiles and aircraft, organizing joint production and development projects. There are also a number of cross invest-ments between American and particularly Japanese corporations (all of which makes the various scenarios of a vicious Japanese and American trade war — or, as often projected, another type of war — somewhat more complex). Usually these deals are made because the development costs are just too burdensome for a single corporation, as in the case of the new generation of passenger aircraft, or because the potential market is too small to fight over. There are also many examples not just of government handouts and subsidies, but also of joint ventures between multinationals and various governments. These are usually part of an industrial or economic policy to share or even transfer technology and manufacturing from one country to another. A case in point is the potential relationship between Taiwan and the struggling McDonnell-Douglas: in exchange for some equity ownership and the movement of manufacturing and technical support to Taiwan, that government will provide much of the funding to develop the projected MD-12 jumbo airliner. A side effect of this deal could be the shutting down of McDonnell-Douglas in Canada.

Government is often a partner in these relationship enterprises, as in the ones described. And government is a partner for specific reasons of state — because of an industrial policy. The idea of the government developing an industrial policy is supposedly part of the discredited notion of government interference in the market. Britain and Canada seemed the last bastions of this so-called free-market approach. Britain, reeling through its worst recession in sixty years, was left with three million unemployed and a manufacturing econ-omy that was withering away. More than two million of its 6.8 million manufacturing jobs were lost over the last decade and manu-facturing now accounts for only 17 per cent of the British gross national product.[10] In Canada, the biggest victim of the recession was the industrial heartland of southern Ontario. *The Economist*'s discus-sion of relationship enterprises emphasizes that they are not merely a product of economics but are driven "by the political necessity of having multiple home bases." What is this notion of "political neces-sity" in this borderless and government-free world? Where does "political necessity" fit into free trade?

The computer, the creation of a single capital market open twenty-four hours a day, all the things that are supposed to make the various national economies passé and the nation-state that developed to create and protect these economies and markets redundant, continue to develop and break through new frontiers. The communications revolution seems to have no end. Yet nothing has developed to replace the state. The central economic principle behind the creation of the "new world order" was the triumph of liberal economics and the unfettered free flow of the market and the demise of the economic functions of the state, and therefore the state itself. This has not happened. Or to be more precise, it has not happened yet.

Rethinking Government

Among economists and social critics who don't believe that the free market always operates for the best and who see a continuing role for the nation-state, there is no shortage of ideas on what that role should be. According to political economist (now U.S. labor secretary) Robert Reich and many others (including Tom Kierans of the C.D. Howe Institute in Canada), the state should invest in the only permanent resource available — a stable labour pool. Thus there is competition both inside and outside the trading bloc for the new high-tech jobs. Those who are the best educated and live in the regions with a superior social and economic infrastructure become the richest and therefore the most prolific consumers. The others get the low-paid jobs and sink.

That countries and regions that cannot offer an educated workforce and a developed infrastructure are destined to engage in low-wage competition with the Third World seems clear enough. Whether it was the fruits of productivity or the fruits of imperialism in which the industrial working class got to share in postwar North America, that formula will no longer work. However, the efficacy of Reich's solutions is restricted to countries that can afford the social investment and are economically positioned to take advantage of it — the United States comes to mind. The United States is also strong enough to make and enforce any trade rules it wants, and it can and often does act to protect its own industries and trading advantages against other countries. As we know from the experience of the domestic Canadian steel industry, build a better mousetrap and the U.S. will beat a path to your door and slap a countervail on it.

In another vein, Gilles Paquet of the University of Ottawa's business school has put forward a vision of the state that is more flexible and participatory, less bureaucratic and authoritarian than the one we are used to.[11] Paquet's "postmodern state" is one that seeks to educate and consult rather than command, that follows the principle of subsidiarity in not trying to do things that are done better at the local level, and that sees its role as being primarily that of a catalyst, partner and moral agent. It is decentralized and organized in modules instead of vertical chains of command.

In many ways, the evolution of the state that Paquet sees is parallel to the evolution of large corporations: "downsizing," the cutting of layers of bureaucracy, less rigid forms of organization, strategic alliances in the form of "virtual corporations"[12] and "relationship enterprises." A state that sets out modest goals for itself and establishes flexible, participatory structures to accomplish them will no doubt be more effective in achieving at least some of these goals than the bureaucratic modern state. But actual models of the postmodern state are only beginning to emerge (notably in Quebec, which provides much of the source material for Paquet's ideas). How all the gaps left by such a "downsized" state will be filled remains to be seen.

Another role we would suggest for national governments is to make multinational corporations more accountable. This can be done only through coordination among different governments across national borders and could usefully involve the supranational bodies these governments have created. Governments at all levels have an interest in putting tax collection on a more businesslike footing, if you will, and also in seeing that communities and environments are not abused by corporate blackmailers who threaten to run off somewhere else. One suggestion along these lines comes from Reginald Weiser, president of an export-oriented Montreal-based, export-oriented firm called Positron Inc., whose product line includes specialized equipment to handle 911 emergency calls:

> North Americans should initiate, by way of example and in conjunction with all industrialized countries, the imposition of restrictions on multinational corporations to prevent them from polluting anywhere in the world above levels established by an international committee from major industrial countries, failing which they would be subject to penalties or restrictions on their operations in the industrialized world. This does not impose hardships on any particular multinational corporation vis-à-vis any other because they would all face the same restrictions. Should this create some competitive advantage somewhere, that would be positive: it would be part of an evolutionary

process which would make nonpolluting activity more competitive, and this would be in the interests of everyone.

The target has to be multinational corporations that are active globally. The only way to affect them is by legislation in countries that are important to them economically. This can effectively transcend all trade deals because, whatever one country does or allows multinationals to do, that multinational would still be penalized elsewhere.[13]

Such an approach — applied not only to pollution but to other evasions of corporate responsibility as well — should find favour with smaller companies that operate at the local level and have less scope for foreign elopement. It should also put some restraints on the undemocratic exercise of the real power held by some corporate behemoths. And it should provide a framework to prevent fiascos such as the spectacular collapse of the Bank of Credit and Commerce International, whose uncertain abode enabled it to escape regulation.

New Forms of Global Reach

We also see a bigger role for nongovernmental, nonbusiness groups such as trade unions and environmental groups. They should be expanding their international alliances just as the corporate sector has done. This can help spur a new internationalist ethos while promoting the more direct exercise of both sovereignty and association.

One of the more memorable images from Canada's free trade election of 1988 is of a Liberal Party television commercial in which Canadian and U.S. negotiators were shown erasing the border between the two countries. The commercial graphically expressed a central theme of the campaign against the Free Trade Agreement: that the fight to defeat free trade was fundamentally a fight to protect Canada's sovereignty.

The need to protect Canadian sovereignty was, in fact, a common thread in the issues raised by liberal-left nationalists from the 1960s through the 1980s. Whether the question was regulating foreign investment, preferential treatment for Canadian magazines, ensuring that Canadian energy supplies were available to Canadians, or preventing massive water-diversion schemes, nationalists based their position on arguments of Canadian sovereignty. The popular appeal of such arguments was broad enough that even Brian Mulroney's Tory government got into the act, claiming that its proposed nuclear submarines were needed to defend Canadian sovereignty, although exactly how they were going to serve that purpose was never clearly demonstrated.

Most if not all of the issues raised by the nationalists are still live ones. But their relationship to the underlying question of sovereignty has changed. In 1992 James Laxer, himself a prominent figure in the Canadian nationalist left, expressed this change in relation to the question of water diversion:

> For Canadians who oppose the export of water to the United States, the situation is somewhat paradoxical. They should certainly not abandon the reduced but still very real ground of national sovereignty. However, national sovereignty, once the centre of the argument, is no longer sufficient in itself. The time has come to shift the burden of the argument away from the rights of states to the broader regional and planetary reasons for opposing interbasin diversions of water. There are strong arguments to be made against the intensive forms of agriculture and industrial mismanagement that create the need for highly expensive water diversions and thus pose a threat to the environment and climate on a wide scale.[14]

The change can also be seen in the second round of the free trade debate, the one about extending free trade to Mexico through NAFTA. Much of the opposition to NAFTA has continued to focus on its effects in Canada, and in particular on the fear that large numbers of Canadian jobs would be lost to take advantage of dramatically lower Mexican wages and weaker labour and environmental standards (see chapter four). However, there has also been a growing recognition among Canadian opponents of NAFTA that its effects on Mexico have to be taken into account as well. Since those effects are likely to be mixed, Canadian opponents of NAFTA have been able to find allies in Mexico, and forming these alliances has been a significant part of their campaign. Visits to Mexico by Council of Canadians chair Maude Barlow, whose liberal-left nationalist credentials are unquestionable, are perhaps the best symbol of this shift in orientation.

The need for the opponents of neoconservative free trade deals to find international allies, and to invoke grounds other than the defence of sovereignty for their arguments, is based on more than just the truism that because capital is international any movement to bring it under control must be international as well. It is also related to the particular nature of the trade deals currently on offer, especially NAFTA and the Uruguay Round of GATT. George Bush was often derided for his self-admitted failure to come to grips with the "vision thing" — something U.S. presidents are expected to have under control. In a 1992 essay, however, *Harper's* magazine contributing editor Walter Russell Mead maintained that Bush did have a vision for America and indeed the world, and that it was articulated in NAFTA and the Uruguay Round:[15]

> The GATT treaty as drafted will essentially establish a new international organization potentially more powerful than the United Nations: a kind of free-trade World Government. . . . The new World Government would be all Bottom Line: a global corporate utopia in which local citizens are toothless, workers' unions are tame or broken, environmentalists and consumer advocates outflanked. It would be a government wherein secrets are kept and conflicts-of-interest are not conflicts at all. It also would be a government in which career insiders will have a greater say than legislators — a circumstance that will elicit no outcry from our current President.

Mead's argument — and it is made by others as well, such as the Ralph Nader organization Public Citizen — is that current trade agreements are less about promoting free trade in the sense of removing tariff barriers than about promoting a regressive social agenda by classifying a variety of social, environmental and consumer protection programs as "unfair subsidies" or "non-tariff barriers" or "technical barriers to trade." In the name of "harmonization," where two countries have different standards for a particular industry or product, the logic of trade agreements makes the less restrictive standard apply to any matters affecting trade between the two countries. And even if the harmful nature of a product can be clearly demonstrated, restrictions on imports of that product are permitted only if it can be shown that there is no other way of controlling its use.

In this way, social legislation that has been achieved in places such as Canada and the United States can be undermined, and social legislation that might be considered in places such as Mexico can be prevented. Corporate interests find trade agreements a better instrument for promoting this agenda than the domestic political process for a variety of reasons. Trade negotiations tend to be secret, and few people outside of business circles pay much attention to them, at least in the United States. And furthermore, once a trade agreement has been signed, it has much wider application and is much more difficult to reverse than a mere domestic regulation or law.

If this was indeed George Bush's vision for the world, and we are convinced that it was, it is a vision that was roundly rejected by American voters in November 1992. The Clinton administration, while not explicitly opposed to international trade agreements, is less enthusiastic about them and has a somewhat different view of what they are about. This view is expressed in its proposed NAFTA side deals aimed at guaranteeing labour and environmental standards, which await ratification at the time of writing. But even if the administration wins approval for its side deals, and even if they prove effective, the GATT agreement is still under consideration and the wider question of the use of trade agreements for regressive social purposes remains.

Probably the most celebrated instance so far of such use of trade agreements has been the 1991 GATT panel ruling that a U.S. law banning imports of tuna caught using methods that kill large numbers of dolphins is an illegal barrier to trade. The Marine Mammal Protection Act (MMPA) was originally passed in 1972 to regulate the methods used by American tuna-fishing boats. However, so long as other countries continued to use the offending methods, the Act's capacity to protect dolphins was limited. "Without extraterritorial impact," noted David Phillips of the San-Francisco-based Earth Island Institute, who presented a brief to the U.S. House of Representatives Subcommittee on Health and the Environment, "the MMPA does little more than disadvantage domestic vessels."

Therefore, Congress amended the MMPA in 1988 to require foreign countries that export tuna to the U.S. to meet marine mammal mortality standards that are no more than 25 per cent higher than U.S. limits. "We do not have the power to regulate foreign fishing operations in foreign waters or on the high seas," said Representative Gerry Studds, chair of the House Subcommittee on Fisheries and Wildlife Conservation and the Environment. "But we *do* have the right to bar our markets to any nation that does not share our concern for the conservation of marine mammals." The law calls for an embargo on tuna from countries that do not meet the standards specified under the MMPA.[16]

The U.S. Commerce Department certified Mexico as one of three countries whose tuna-fishing practices failed to meet "dolphin-safe" standards in 1990. However, the Bush administration failed to impose an embargo on Mexican tuna, and it was only after an environmental coalition took the administration to court and won a series of favourable rulings that an embargo was imposed in March 1991. Anticipating the embargo, Mexico had already filed a GATT challenge against the MMPA. In August, a GATT dispute resolution panel consisting of three officials from countries not involved in the dispute ruled in Mexico's favour. According to the ruling, a country is not allowed under GATT to discriminate on the basis of the way a product is harvested or produced. Nor can it take any action aimed at protecting health or the environment outside its borders if that action could have an impact on trade.

Among other health and environmental measures that have been struck down or challenged as trade barriers are Canadian pesticide limits, Canadian incentives to nonferrous metal producers to install pollution control devices to combat acid rain, a U.S. ban on asbestos, a European Community ban on beef hormones, and measures undertaken by various countries to restrict tobacco use.[17] In cases where GATT has been involved, the provisions in question have been ones agreed to during the Tokyo Round, which concluded in 1979 and was the first to deal significantly with non-tariff barriers. A Uruguay Round agreement — still on the negotiating table at the time of writing — would substantially broaden the scope of GATT's struggle against non-tariff barriers and expand the range of health, environmental and consumer standards that could be challenged as barriers to trade.

If dolphins seem like improbable candidates for entanglement in international trade agreements, the involvement of mothers' milk appears even more far-fetched. However, breastfeeding advocacy organizations have found that deals such as GATT and the Canada-U.S. Free Trade Agreement represent an increasingly serious obstacle to their efforts to control the marketing practices of large and often multinational infant formula corporations.

Thus, in the summer of 1991 a Health and Welfare Canada official told the Toronto-based Infant Feeding Action Coalition (INFACT Canada) that the Canada-U.S. Free Trade Agreement "superseded" the World Health Organization's decade-old International Code of Marketing of Breast-Milk Substitutes.[18] And at a "breastfeeding promotion" meeting sponsored by Health and Welfare's Health Promotion Directorate, the WHO Code of Marketing was described as a restriction on infant formula manufacturers' rights to compete freely in the marketplace. The implication of these statements was that it was pointless for breastfeeding advocates such as INFACT Canada to continue their campaign to require the formula manufacturers to comply with the WHO code.

Elisabeth Sterken, the national coordinator of INFACT Canada, describes the WHO code, adopted in 1981, as "the culmination of extraordinary efforts by governments, international agencies, activists, women's groups and religious organizations working together to solve a global problem."[19] The problem is that despite the well-established health benefits of breastfeeding, many parents are persuaded to bottle feed their children through the marketing practices of the large formula manufacturers.[20] Perhaps the most invidious of these practices is the supply of free formula samples to new parents through hospitals and doctors' offices. Such free samples, along with advertising aimed directly at the public and other practices, are proscribed in the WHO code.

Formula companies can use both the Canada-U.S. FTA and GATT — with their tendency to define such things as labelling requirements and marketing restrictions as trade barriers — as tools to undermine the WHO code. A more expansive GATT deal will give greater power to an international agency called the Codex Alimentarius Commission, which sets the food standards for GATT. Unlike WHO and UNICEF, which have actively promoted breastfeeding, Codex Alimentarius is closely linked to the formula industry and especially to its leading firm, the Swiss-based multinational Nestlé.[21]

In response to the global nature of the issue, breastfeeding advocacy organizations have been working together across national borders since the late 1970s and are linked in the International Baby Food Action Network (IBFAN). Their activities include trying to monitor and influence the World Health Organization — at WHO meetings corporate representatives sit in one gallery and representatives of nongovernmental organizations (NGOs) sit across from them in another — and coordinating an international boycott of Nestlé in protest against its formula marketing practices. In December 1991, concerned about the direction international trade agreements were taking, representatives from Canada, the United States and Mexico set up IBFAN Trade Watch as a coalition for action on trade issues.

Breastfeeding advocacy organizations, like other NGOs, still spend most of their time trying to change attitudes and influence the policies of governments in their home countries, but their international activities are an increasingly significant aspect of their work. In no sense do the international networks of NGOs represent a serious counterweight to the far more highly developed international networks of corporations. But they do represent a recognition of the need for such a counterweight, and perhaps an early indication of where it might emerge.

It should not be surprising that the emergence of an international nongovernmental organization network has been most conspicuous in the area of environment and development, now seen as closely interrelated concerns, for nowhere else has it become quite so clear that the questions at issue are global ones. In the early days of the modern environmental movement, in the 1960s and 1970s, the issues the movement took on were often local in nature — a toxic waste dump here, a dying lake there, a factory spewing pollutants into the atmosphere somewhere else. The movement won its victories by preserving a forest or stopping a company from polluting a river. "Think globally, act locally" was its catchy and rather comforting slogan.

Even at this stage, there were problems — such as acid rain in eastern Canada, largely caused by industrial emissions in the midwestern United States — that could not be neatly contained within national units. In the mid-1980s, however, public consciousness began to focus on two environmental problems that not only crossed national borders but were clearly global: damage to the ozone layer and global warming. In coming to grips with these problems, action at a local level, or even at the level of a national state, is not enough. They require concerted action by international organizations, governments, corporations and citizens.

Furthermore, because they are largely products of First World affluence, they raise the question of international development and the worldwide distribution of wealth. If the planet cannot withstand the impact of too many more cars, refrigerators and air conditioners, do the masses of the South have to give up wanting these Northern comforts? Will the North give up some of its comforts so that they can be shared more equitably? Or will new technologies solve the problem? The 1987 report of the World Commission on Environment and Development, the Brundtland Commission, provided a catchphrase for what was needed: *sustainable development*[22] (like most catchphrases, it meant almost whatever its user wanted it to mean). Meanwhile, governments and NGOs began to prepare for the United

Nations Conference on Environment and Development, the "Earth Summit," in Rio de Janeiro in 1992.

The Earth Summit turned out to be different in important respects from previous international conferences, and one of these respects was the way in which NGOs participated. Traditionally, an NGO would be involved in the preparation for an international conference by providing input to the position of its national government. One United Nations Development Program document issued about a year and a half before the Earth Summit suggested that the expertise of NGOs was essentially at the local level, and it was at that level that they could make their most effective contribution.

The NGOs resisted this view of their role. They were interested in linking the local and the global, and in working together across national boundaries. Months of intensive preparation involving hundreds of NGOs from all over the world helped develop some common understandings. At the Earth Summit itself, NGO participation was focused primarily on the International NGO Forum (INGOF), which took place within the context of the Global Forum, an unofficial sideshow to the meeting of government delegations that constituted the summit proper.

At INGOF the NGOs concluded thirty-nine treaties covering a wide variety of topics: trade and sustainable development, consumption and lifestyle, poverty, debt, transnational corporations, alternative economic models and others. Each treaty contains a statement of the problem as seen by the NGOs along with suggestions for NGO action and further cooperation. Thus, the treaty on debt contains eight "strategies for action." One of these is to "undertake joint campaigns against the debt, building on case studies from the regions of Latin America, Africa and Asia. These campaigns will be addressed at local, provincial, national, regional and international levels. The campaigns will include a policy statement on illegal and fraudulent debts that will reinforce demands for the cancellation of the debt." Another is to "develop joint policy positions on the debt regarding freedom of information, transfer of resources, accountability and public participation in policy making; press for the democratization of the dialogue between creditor institutions and governments so as to include social organizations and NGOs. These policy positions will be addressed to multilateral lending agencies, creditor governments, relevant official institutions, social movements and the NGO community."[23]

With hundreds of people working on each treaty, meeting in tents over a few days and engaged in proceedings in four languages with simultaneous translation, the quality of the treaties was admittedly uneven. Even Peter Padbury of the Ottawa-based Canadian Council for International Cooperation, who has been deeply involved in the treaty-making process and its aftermath, admits that some of them are a "mess." Nevertheless, they represent a significant step towards sustained NGO cooperation on a global level.

According to Padbury, three underlying — and in some ways rather surprising — principles characterized the vision of the NGOs' work that emerged from Rio: a view of themselves not simply as critics but as cocreators of new models, a commitment to link the local and the global, and a determination to carry out this work not by setting up new institutions but through more fluid "networks" and "processes" instead.

The most optimistic thing that can be said about this work is that it is in its very early stages. Padbury suggests that it may take ten to twenty years before NGOs work out a coherent alternative strategy on issues of environment and development. Another challenge is to develop more of a mass base for NGO positions and activities. The treaties often speak of "NGOs and social movements": the distinction is between organizations that often possess considerable expertise and strategic sophistication but are generally small, self-mandated and not accountable to anybody (the NGOs) and ones that are large, mass-based and democratic but are often unable to see beyond immediate goals (the social movements). The steps towards global cooperation that developed out of Rio were in fact taken by NGOs, but much less so by social movements. If a genuinely effective alternative to corporate globalization is ever to emerge from this sector, it will be necessary to bridge the gap between the two.

A year after Rio, a different grouping of NGOs from around the world gathered in an effort to influence the direction of another major international conference, this time the UN Conference on Human Rights in Vienna. Human rights, now also viewed as a world issue (although one where the complex relationship among global standards, national sovereignty, and cultural and religious traditions remains to be worked out), is an area where NGOs have been especially active at the international level. According to Montreal human rights lawyer and scholar Irwin Cotler, "It might seem paradoxical to attribute a 'legislative' role to Non-Governmental Organizations; but increasingly, and in the international arena in particular, NGO's are playing a formative role in the initiation, drafting, interpretation, and application of international human rights agreements and standard-setting generally."[24]

Like *sustainable development, civil society* is a phrase that has been widely heard only since the late 1980s; before that it was largely restricted to adepts of the thought of the influential Italian Communist leader Antonio Gramsci, who used it to describe the various sectors of society outside the state. Its increasing popularity reflects the growing sense that governments are not the only legitimate actors — either within their own borders or on the world stage. We have cautioned against the fashionable idea that governments no longer have, or deserve to have, any significant role, but we do not question the proposition that their role has changed and will continue to change. The sovereignty of governments (which implies the sovereignty of the people who elect them, even if only indirectly and imperfectly) has been undermined primarily as a result of international corporate power. But if there is to be a humane and democratic alternative to corporate globalization, it will in all likelihood be constructed within civil society, and at least to an extent within international civil society.

Chapter 4

The Growth of Trade Blocs

Think back to North America in the 1950s, and chances are the images that spring to mind will seem unreal. There was Ike, taking precious moments away from his golf habit to attend to matters in the White House, Uncle Louis doing his real-life personification of the sleepwalking Canadian prime minister, everyone's dad driving to work in a blur of tail fins, mom staying behind in the suburban dream home to look after the kids, the fallout shelter in the basement, and Elvis as King.

We can chuckle now, but at the time this was not too shabby a situation when viewed from afar. Europe had recovered from the worst of wartime devastation, but living standards were low and the future looked cloudy. The United States, on the other hand, was a country that had succeeded. It had prospered during the war, its economy continued to grow robustly, its industry and agriculture dominated world trade, it had billions of dollars to recycle abroad and, even if its political leaders and cultural icons seemed un-fathomably hokey, it was a country that exuded optimism and con-fidence in the future.

The European Model

Europe was the continent that had invented the modern nation-state, and this creation had entered into deadly conflict with economic development. It seemed that no country felt it could be taken seri-ously as a sovereign state unless it had, for starters, its own integrated steel industry and its own international airline. (We will return to both of these sectors, along with automobiles and agriculture, in chapter six.) These industries, often small-scale and inefficient, could survive only with protection. An assortment of tariffs and other trade barriers were hobbling Europe's economic growth, while in the U.S. the products of industry could move across the breadth of a continent without so much as a customs officer's stamp.

Jean Monnet, the French statesman and former brandy merchant whose ideas helped inspire European integration, pointed often to the U.S. model and warned that Europe would have to keep pace or risk becoming an economic backwater. The first big postwar steps towards eliminating trade obstacles in Western Europe came with the signing of the Treaty of Paris in 1951. This treaty paved the way for the creation of the European Steel and Coal Community, and later the signing of the 1957 Treaty of Rome, which superseded it. With the Treaty of Rome, the European Economic Community was brought into being with six countries as members, joined in later decades by six others.

National jealousies and rivalries did not vanish with the creation of what became known simply as the European Community. Nor did ideological conflicts disappear. Nevertheless, the basic idea of the EC achieved a remarkable consensus among governments of varying ideological stripes, including social democrats, Christian democrats, conservatives, liberals and Labourites.

The longer-term ambitions of the EC extend well beyond trade policy to encompass monetary, foreign and social policy. A treaty signed by member governments in the Dutch town of Maastricht in 1991 laid out a detailed path for post-1992 changes that were to take place following the removal of remaining barriers to intra-Community movements of goods, capital and labour. The early going was not marked by conspicuous success. The Maastricht treaty was put to national referendums in Ireland, Denmark and France. In Ireland, a substantial net recipient of Community funds, support was strong. But in Denmark, the treaty was narrowly rejected the first time around and was approved in a second referendum only after Denmark won exemptions from some of its provisions. And in France, where the most visible opponents of ratification were the Communist Party and the professional xenophobes of the extreme right (not the most cheerful of bedfellows), the treaty won only by a tiny margin.

In foreign policy, the EC showed its true mettle when it proved incapable of playing any useful role in the conflicts in the former Yugoslavia. Monetary policy fell into a similar shambles late in 1992 when several EC members allowed sharp devaluations of their currencies, abandoning commitments under the European Monetary System to keep fluctuations within narrow bands. Meanwhile, the Maastricht-mandated process towards a single European currency began springing leaks and looked as if it might be delayed well beyond the target dates.

Currency union has important consequences in both symbolic and practical terms. Banknotes and coins are among the most powerful of national icons, and subsuming them under a pan-European currency unit would mark the disappearance of something deeply imbedded in the national psyche. This is especially so among the British, never the most enthusiastic of Europeans, and among the Germans, who are proud of the enduring strength of the deutsche mark and would rather not see it replaced by something less solid (even if, as seems likely, the new European central bank is cast as a continuation of their own Bundesbank in its anti-inflation virtue and independence from direct political control). In practical terms, the maintenance of separate currencies makes it more expensive to trade or travel between European countries because of time lost and commissions paid in changing money. In the U.S. only one currency is used across a huge internal market, and this is viewed as an American strength.

Just as support for European integration has crossed ideological lines, so has opposition. Sore points among EC opponents run the gamut from unaccountable Brussels bureaucrats (a favourite Thatcherite target) to the preposterous Common Agricultural Policy, which swallows one-third of the Community budget, keeps European food prices high, creates huge unsaleable surpluses of agricultural products, and hurts farmers elsewhere when portions of these surpluses are dumped (see chapter six).

The most vociferous opposition to the EC has come from nationalists reluctant to give up even small amounts of national sovereignty. The EC is based on the notion that certain matters can be handled best at the supranational level and that this requires the pooling of some aspects of sovereign authority, with their execution placed in the hands of the Brussels-based European Commission and other Community bodies. Not everyone likes this idea.

Some nationalists also perceive threats to the distinct national cultures that are such a deeply ingrained part of Europe; they say European integration could put a horrid homogeneous blob in their place. Countering these fears is the enthusiasm for supranationalism shown by national minorities such as Scots or Catalans, who see in the lessening of nation-state sovereignty a partial lifting of the weight of historical oppression and a chance to enhance their autonomy and cultural expression without the risk of economic or political isolation.

Significant portions of the European left also have been wary of the EC, seeing it as a capitalist club that places lids on the promotion of broader social interests. Certainly, none of the EC member governments can be described as anticapitalist: they all accept, with varying degress of enthusiasm, the idea of a market economy. Nor can there be much doubt that economic integration has widened the scope for multinational corporate activity in Europe for firms based both in Europe and abroad.

Of course, in encouraging the growth of capitalism, the EC has merely reflected the will of elected national governments across Western Europe. If, in elections to national parliaments and to the European Parliament, citizens chose majorities favouring ideas that deviated sharply from capitalist orthodoxy, this would eventually be reflected in EC institutions and policies. However, the process of integration does have the effect of taking some powers away from elected national governments and entrenching certain practices at the Community level, where they may be more difficult to reverse or change. The Maastricht treaty, for example, commits all EC members to anti-inflation policies and low deficits — tying the hands of a future government that might want to follow a different path.

Another cause for skepticism about European integration has been migration policy. With the removal of remaining legal barriers to intra-EC labour mobility at the end of 1992, citizens of any EC country now have the right to settle and work anywhere in the EC. In particular, the so-called Schengen countries (all the EC members except Ireland, Britain and Denmark), which together are pursuing a "fast track" to European integration, now constitute in theory, and to an only slightly lesser degree in practice, a passport-free zone. This has not spurred any great wave of migration — partly because most EC countries have been loath to extend citizenship to immigrants from outside the EC. Germany and France both have threatened to impose draconian new measures against immigration — Germany seeking to stanch the influx of Slavs and Turks, and France's new right-wing government hoping to stop more Arabs or West Africans from entering. Because of the porous nature of European borders, the immigration concerns of individual countries become Community concerns as well.

If Turks, North Africans, Gypsies or Poles can no longer be stopped at the borders of Germany or France, they have to be stopped at a new border surrounding the relatively favoured EC as a whole — especially at a time of economic stagnation, high unemployment and rising xenophobia in a number of European countries. Since Europe is in any case no longer accepting significant numbers of immigrants for economic purposes, the new effort at closing the borders through "harmonization" has been aimed primarily at asylum-seekers. Germany's decision in May 1993 to amend its constitution to limit the right to asylum was a significant step in this process. James Hathaway, associate director of the Centre for Refugee Studies at Toronto's York University, writes:

> Fearful that a continuing commitment to refugee protection threatens the viability of a union premised on external closure, states have taken the facile approach of elaborating a policy of generalized deterrence: all persons seeking entry from less developed states — whether or not they have a valid claim to refugee status — will be stigmatized as potential threats to European communal well-being, and their prospects for ingress consequently constrained. Under the guise of "harmonization," European governments have effectively renounced their commitment to an interregional system of asylum.

> Equally ominous, the procedural context within which this common policy of deterrence has been devised breaks with the tradition of elaborating norms of refugee law through an open and politically accountable process. Opting to collaborate within a covert network of intergovernmental decision-making bodies spawned by the economic integration process itself, governments have dedicated themselves to the avoidance of national, international and supranational scrutiny grounded in the human rights standards inherent in refugee law.[1]

While the European Parliament and Council of Europe have taken a more humanitarian view of asylum policy than European governments, they have been effectively excluded from decision-making in this area. Here again the Schengen countries, operating through intergovernmental agreements, have taken the lead.

On the other hand, left-wing support for European integration has been encouraged by the Community's social charter (or social chapter, as it was called at Maastricht), an interesting idea whose time has evidently come but whose application looks uncertain. It was advocated in 1988 by European Commission president Jacques Delors and adopted in 1989 at a meeting of the European Council, where eleven of the twelve EC member countries (Thatcher's Britain being the noisy and obvious dissenter) gave their approval. Not everyone was happy with the result: the original concept had been watered down to win British support, without in the end achieving that aim. The version that appears in the Maastricht treaty (with Tory Britain still defiantly opting out) covers such areas as free movement of workers, freedom of collective bargaining, health and safety protection in the workplace, and sexual equality in employment.

In his 1991 book *Inventing Europe*, James Laxer noted that the support of European governments for the social charter appeared "massive and impressive" across political lines, but that "once one looked beyond the principles and platitudes to the details of an action program," this support may have reflected tactical considerations above anything else:

> One reason German Christian Democrats were inclined to support a social charter was that they were concerned about the risk that corporations might be tempted to escape high-wage Germany with its tough environmental provisions, its expensive social programs, and its stiff regulations about laying off employees in favour of the low-wage and relatively unregulated European south. For exactly the obverse reasons, Felipe González, the Socialist prime minister of Spain, did not really want a social charter with teeth because he looked forward to many of those "runaway" plants from northern Europe relocating in his country.[2]

But Laxer also outlined the logic behind a social charter and the appeal it could hold for many Euroskeptics on the left:

> Even though the charter would not have much immediate effect on the obligations of business, the principles enshrined in it could have serious implications for the long term. For the future, the charter held out the prospect that it would be much more difficult for enterprises to shift their operations from one EC state to another to seek the advantages of a less regulated environment. The ability of multinational businesses to move from state to state and to play jurisdictions off, one against another, has been one of the great advantages of capital versus labour and government in the present global environment. The social charter established a basis for redressing the balance within the EC. As European union proceeds, both economically

and politically, the likelihood is that the action programs associated with the social charter will become more ambitious.[3]

The need for a social charter — along with the danger inherent in its
not applying to all European states — was highlighted in early 1993
by the decision of Hoover, the European subsidiary of the American
Maytag Corporation, to close vacuum cleaner production in one
small plant and consolidate it in another that has what from management's point of view is a more amenable labour contract.

For Canadians and Americans, Hoover's decision seemed like no
big deal. This sort of thing happens frequently on this side of the
Atlantic; it is, after all, the nature of competition. The market is not
merely the test of the entrepreneur but also the test of the artisan and
worker. North Americans seem to understand these things and participate in the competition and the "downsizing" with a fatalism that
now approaches morbid zeal. General Motors plants vie with one
another in rollbacks and concessions. Municipal, state and provincial
jurisdictions compete with incentives, tax holidays and plain give-
aways. In early 1993 the trade union at a Mack Truck assembly plant
in the United States voted to accept wage concessions if management
agreed to end production at a plant in Oakville, Ontario, and consolidate operations in the U.S. This dubious show of labour solidarity
hardly merited a news item in the local press although twice as many
workers were involved as at the Hoover plant in France.

Is North American equanimity a result of longer experience at free
trade? Hardly; the Europeans have been working on free trade since
the collapse of the Roman Empire. Ironically, the Glasgow plant in
which Hoover is consolidating production is very close to the place
of Adam Smith's birth. Is it because the Europeans are more recent
arrivals at the point of economic stagnation and constriction? This
may be a more promising line of inquiry, if for no other reason than
that Britain, and the old industrial belt around Glasgow in particular,
have been trying to cope with the fallout from the Thatcher "economic miracle" for years. Desperation may breed inventive grovel-
ling.

The spokespeople for the union at Hoover's Scottish plant say they
have nothing to be ashamed of: it is simply that the work rules are
more "flexible" in Scotland than in France. *The Economist* naturally
sees nothing wrong with the move either.[4] It acquits the British
government of any wrongdoing in that its bribe to Hoover was no
larger than the French government's proposed aid package to the

company. While noting that the furor in France had much to do with the election campaign then in progress, the magazine also warned of the proposed move by a German television manufacturer from France to Austria:

> For as long as the politicians howl every time a company makes such a decision, the single market will live dangerously. . . . The free movement of capital and labour is what the single market is supposed to be all about. Hoover has done nothing wrong. To remain competitive in what is fast becoming a global business, the company feels it must concentrate vacuum-cleaner production in Europe in a single plant.[5]

In any event, no big deal. Merely the closure of a small plant in Dijon with a loss of 600 jobs. Still, the move aroused the Quai d'Orsay and provoked the foreign minister to declare it "a very serious incident." It is serious because of the portent of other Hoovers to come and the attitude it reveals of every country for itself — also manifested in the 1992 currency crisis. It may well be that the fabled European unity is something whose time has not so much come as already gone.

In the heady days leading up to the Maastricht summit of 1991, *Newsweek* wrote about how Europe went from Eurosclerosis in the recession of the early 1980s through Europhoria in 1985 with the proposal to eliminate all trade barriers by 1992 to the new Euroreal-ism as everyone got down to the nitty gritty.[6] Perhaps now it can be called Europression as a bankrupt Britain not only refused to agree to the social charter but also was unable to defend the pound and went through a massive devaluation. The Hoover incident presages less a united market than an incipient trade war, although such a conclusion may be premature.

Within the European bloc, as in America and to a lesser extent in Asia, there are protectionist tensions and competitions, which in difficult economic times make for situations such as Hoover and the political fallout that ensues. But there are also tensions relating to joint and interstate cooperative ventures. A case in point is the DAF automotive corporation, an Anglo-Dutch-Belgian firm that would be a candidate for bankruptcy under most conditions. If it is to be bailed out, who will do the bailing — Britain, Belgium or the Netherlands? Britain seems to be prepared to see the Leyland part go under, but that would mean that any restructuring would exclude any of the 6,000 jobs remaining in Britain.

On the other hand, it could be sold. The only and therefore logical buyer is a Japanese corporation. This would conceivably give Nissan a toehold in the European market. But while this solution could salvage some British jobs, it would not be welcomed by France, Italy and especially Germany, which have major automobile industries they need to protect. And so it goes through nuclear energy, oil and resource development (particularly in the former Soviet Union), aerospace development and the Airbus consortium, which cannot afford to develop a new generation of aircraft by itself. Can it both compete and cooperate with Boeing? What kind of technology transfers are required to keep its potential customers in Asia on board?

Or perhaps the best description of Europe 1993 is Euroreich. Prior to the Maastricht summit, former West German chancellor Helmut Schmidt advised Britain and other members of the EC:

> The British have a choice to make between the European currency unit [Ecu] and the deutsche mark. . . . If they opt for a single currency within the common market they will have a very good chance to develop the City of London as one of the world's most important financial centres. They would be able to draw on the vast future pool of German capital in the European currency unit. . . . [If they] maintain their monetary sovereignty . . . the British will wake up to the fact that any importance of sterling will have evaporated. . . . *Even more than it does today, the Bundesbank will then direct monetary policy purely on the basis of German interests.* (emphasis added)

Schmidt went on:

> The French, Dutch, Italians, Poles, Hungarians and all the rest are faced with a clear choice. On one hand they can opt for progress in European integration . . . or they can choose to hesitate and find that Germany, in ten years, is too powerful a neighbour to handle.[7]

It should be noted that Schmidt's warning that the foreplay was about to end came when the economy in Europe was expanding, the British and the Reichmanns could dream of a revitalized London financial centre, and Europe including Britain still had the apparent ability to make a choice — even if it was something like Hobson's Choice. But those heady days are gone. In a constricting market, the British and Italians have had to devalue their currencies and get out of the club (see chapter two), while others are hanging on by their fingernails. The dream of some great European commonwealth has receded in the face of the prospect of a powerful Germany dominating the whole continent — not the original six or the twelve, but the new Europe from the Atlantic to the Urals and beyond.

Yet it is a very overextended Germany. While the high interest rates of the Bundesbank strangle the other European economies and even undermine any American recovery, they also threaten to destabilize Germany itself. The jackboots along the cobblestones of old German cities may not presage the fifth Reich or a return to the Weimar Republic, but they certainly place some stress on the new carefully cultivated image of Germany as the sacred home of peace, power and corporatism.

The North American Derivative

There are clear similarities between the concept of European unity and the other trading blocs now emerging. They are fundamentally restrictive of global trade, and Europe is aligning itself both to restrict and to do battle with America and Japan. And within these blocs a dominant country or force is established. North America means the United States, the Pacific Rim means Japan and, as Helmut Schmidt pointed out, those Ecus are really deutsche marks and you may look for Europe but will only see the German multistate.

However, comparing Europe with North America, some equally striking differences stand out. First, the chief instrument of North American integration, the North American Free Trade Agreement, is in a more rudimentary state, comparable to where the EC was three decades ago. Second, NAFTA is not envisaged as a political grouping, and at this stage there are no plans to establish the range of community institutions that exist in Europe. The only body being set up to deal specifically with NAFTA affairs is a dispute settlement panel — a far cry from the commission, council, parliament and sundry other bodies handling EC affairs. Third, while Germany is obviously the single most powerful member of the EC (even if France pretends to be the single most powerful member), not even Germany's economic might comes anywhere close to the more than 85 per cent of economic output that the United States accounts for in the trilateral North American grouping. Fourth, NAFTA does little to promote labour mobility. And the list continues.

Another fundamental difference, which James Laxer stresses in his 1993 book *False God*, is that the U.S. is unlikely to agree to any EC-style pooling of sovereignty.[8] If the U.S. did start leaning that way, Canada and Mexico would want to run for cover, for they too would have to pool sovereignty, and we know who would end up exercising it in their place. It is hard also to envisage a North American monetary union. As desirable as it might be in strictly economic terms to have a single continent-wide currency, that currency could only be the U.S. dollar: the Americans wouldn't have it any other way, nor should they. But this would be a bitter pill for Canadians and Mexicans to swallow, if only for the silly reason that they like their banknotes to have different colours; it would not be the same as the nationality-neutral European currency unit.

What of a social charter? So soon after the levelling-down mentality of twelve years of Republican rule, it was hard to imagine a U.S. administration agreeing to anything that might strike the left as progressive. But, lo and behold, the Clintonites were holding up NAFTA ratification to get side deals aimed at assuring enforcement of labour standards and environmental codes. At the time of writing there was no way even of surmising where this might lead, but it did show a willingness to consider these issues even if the intent of this initiative was essentially protectionist. (In a delicious irony, this put Michael Wilson in the unfamiliar position of expressing concerns about sovereignty when he insisted the U.S. should not be empowered to invoke labour or environmental issues as a justification for disrupting trade because this would represent interference with the sovereignty of Canada or Mexico.)

Trade blocs are tangling with questions of how far they should venture, not only in jurisdictional terms but in geographic terms as well. NAFTA, under a hub-and-spoke scenario envisaged in Washington, would grow to encompass most of South America (with Chile probably the first of the new spokes). The EC has been debating whether it should go "deeper" — consolidating and expanding its areas of responsibility — before going "broader" and admitting new members. New entrants would include the current membership of the European Free Trade Association (Austria, Switzerland, Sweden, Finland, Norway, Iceland) minus one or two holdouts. East Germany was a *de facto* EC member even before German reunification. The countries to follow — though probably not for years to come —

would include Poland, Hungary, the Czech Republic, Slovakia and, possibly, Slovenia, the richest and most tranquil of the former Yugoslav republics. Turkey's interest in joining has been largely unrequited, but its day could come too.

The EC, like so many other Western bodies, still has not come fully to terms with the end of the Cold War. Before the demise of the Moscow-centred Comecon trade bloc, the question of admitting Eastern countries simply didn't arise except in the context of some vague associate status. Now that most countries in Eastern Europe were struggling to build market economies, they were hoping to see the welcome mat rolled out fairly soon or, failing that, at least to enjoy relatively unimpeded access to Western European markets. But they have been cheated of this in the early going by protectionist pressures within the EC.

By now it should be apparent that it's no easy task to build coherent trade blocs, and this fact plays into the hands of those who say it isn't desirable either. Even where the intention of a trade bloc is merely to ease the flow of goods and capital, myriad other considerations come creeping in, as both sides in the NAFTA debate are already well aware.

Mexico as the Issue

Foreign bogeymen have been part and parcel of the American political arsenal almost any time the need has arisen to frighten the populace or to assign blame for an assortment of evils. For decades the Soviet Union fit the bill admirably, being the very embodiment of evil. Here was the perfect bogeyman: big, powerful, dangerous, unredeemably alien, fiendishly devoted to the imposition of political and economic structures that denied the supremacy of mom, apple pie and much else.

Other bogeymen have filled bit roles in Washington rather effectively. Fidel Castro has been a perennial; Muammar Qadafi and the late Ayatollah Khomeini have also helped out. Ronald Reagan even tried to get mileage out of such unlikely threats as Daniel Ortega of Nicaragua and Maurice Bishop of Grenada. George Bush, visibly annoyed when his former pals Manuel Noriega and Saddam Hussein went astray, resorted to heavy demonization as a prelude to military action.

The end of the Cold War has dealt a serious blow to demonmongers, and the rise of Islamic militancy has provided only a partial respite. With the demise of the Soviet Union and the defanging of most of its surrogates, military and ideological threats have become harder to conjure up. Attention has turned instead to North America's economic rivals.

The new bogeymen are countries whose products fill the homes and garages of American consumers. Most are fellow practitioners of capitalism who have twisted the rules to their own advantage, largely by producing things people want and selling at prices they are willing to pay. Japan-bashing has become fair sport in Washington and a solid tradition in Detroit and the rest of the Midwestern rust belt. Other East Asian countries with big trade surpluses are also coming in for their share of abuse. Up to now this anti-Asia sentiment has taken weaker root in Canada, just as anti-Sovietism had a less virulent following here. But when it comes to Mexico-bashing, Canadian opponents of free trade seem prepared to rough it up with the best of them.

Canada's Mexico-bashers, by and large, stand poles apart from the old-fashioned reactionaries who used to rail against the Red Menace. Most would consider themselves politically progressive; they would insist that it's not Mexico as a country or Mexican workers who are the targets of their campaign, but rather Mexican bosses and government officials whose scant regard for human and environmental concerns is by now a matter of broad public knowledge in Canada.

The most basic worry of anti-NAFTA activists, and nobody can fault them for it, remains the potential loss of Canadian jobs. But their message all too often seems redolent of the xenophobic nastiness that tainted old-time Commie-bashing even if a sympathetic veil is placed on it. Mexicans are a different sort of people, or so the gist of many unfortunate arguments seems to run; they work for slave wages and those in charge don't meet civilized Canadian standards and so Canada should restrict entry of their goods. Typical of this line of argument is an article signed by Greenpeace Québec contending that Mexico is among those countries that "cannot allow themselves to refuse any industry as polluting as it may be, and where people are dying of hunger and are ready to endure the worst working conditions and toxicity just to survive."[9] In fact, Mexican levels of caloric intake are quite high, and workplaces with high levels of toxicity often have trouble retaining permanent employees.

Those who argue against NAFTA on grounds that Mexican standards are different from Canadian ones seem to ignore the fact that if

Canada traded only with people whose standards are just the same as its own, there would be nobody to trade with.

At first glance, Mexico is an unlikely economic bogeyman. For reasons of historical mistrust and economic backwardness, Mexico has been slow to develop a strong exporting tradition — in spite of proximity to the vast U.S. market that should make Mexicans the envy of exporters in countless other countries. A few signatures on a trade agreement won't change this overnight. By contrast, aggressive trading countries such as Taiwan and South Korea have done well in North America without the benefit of either geographic proximity or a free trade accord, and will continue to do so. NAFTA will not make Mexico suddenly resemble an Asian tiger.

Changes are occurring in select areas. The foreign-based automakers that began assembling vehicles in Mexico decades ago under ultraprotectionist rules sheltering them rigidly from outside competition were long content to serve only the national market; more recently they have become major exporters. But their export performance — up to now, anyway — has not been part of any broad general pattern in Mexican industry.

Ever since U.S. invaders annexed nearly half of Mexico's territory in the 1840s, the country has guarded its sovereignty with intense jealousy, despite some odd twists and turns. Most foreign-owned property was expropriated or destroyed during the Revolution of the 1910s, and the entire oil industry was nationalized in 1938. Until quite recently, restrictions on foreign investment in Mexico were among the tightest in the capitalist world. This has begun to change under the current wave of economic liberalization; a fresh welcome mat has been laid out for foreign investment. It now seems that Mexican export drives will be directed largely from outside.

Foreign-owned multinational companies are not the only major industrial exporters in Mexico, but they are among the most successful, in part because they are run by people who are attuned to international competition. Mexican-owned industries, with some notable exceptions, have tended to sell mostly in the national market. Protected for many years by high tariff and quota walls, they could turn out shoddy, overpriced goods and still sell almost everything they produced. Some of these same companies are neglecting even now to prepare themselves for the advent of freer trade. Many firms — and their employees — will fall by the wayside because of a failure to develop and market quality goods at competitive prices.

Free trade is no bed of roses on either side of the border, but neither is protectionism, which has to take the blame for many of Mexico's industrial woes. Two conceptions of Mexican society are coming face to face. One is sluggish, folkloric, backward-looking and patronizing; the other is brisk, rootless, unpredictable and patronizing. Neither offers the certitudes or the comfort that most people tend to crave. Only one offers serious prospects of long-term economic improvement for a majority of the population, and it will exact some painful sacrifices. Needless to say, these sacrifices will not be shared equally. Economic justice is easier to pronounce than to achieve, and grotesque gaps between rich and poor have been part of Mexican tradition since Aztec times. Free trade will not make these gaps disappear. But if a pair of Mexican public opinion polls taken in early 1993 are to be believed, many Mexicans hope that a more dynamic and open economic system could narrow them.

Mexico is still lumped in as part of the Third World, a term that embraces countries at vastly different levels of economic development. By most measures, Mexico is clearly among the wealthier in this group. Using market exchange rates, it in fact is wealthier than much of ex-Communist Eastern Europe (in the former Second World). But in areas such as public education and social levelling, Mexico still has far to go. Figures citing average income levels often conceal more than they show. If a man has one leg in boiling water and the other packed in ice, then on average his legs should be quite comfortable.

There remain other gaps as well. The slow-moving, knee-deep stream that Americans misleadingly call the Rio Grande (and Mexicans just as implausibly call the Rio Bravo) not only forms the border between Texas and Mexico but also separates the so-called First and Third worlds. The U.S.-Mexico border is the only place on Earth where a wealthy industrial power abuts directly on what, in less correct times, was called an underdeveloped country.

The busiest border crossing in North America is the one between Tijuana and San Ysidro, California, just south of San Diego, and it is here that the contrast between north and south is at its sharpest. It is Texas, however, that forms the longest stretch of Mexico's northern boundary. Texas is renowned for its brash millionaires, but it has a higher proportion of poor people than most other U.S. states, and it is notoriously stingy with social spending.

Southern Texas is not one of the more appealing parts of the continent. Its barren landscapes and ubiquitous dust, its scruffy bungalows and trailer courts, its bleak towns and shabby commercial strips all form a depressing picture. And yet it may look downright glitzy to someone living only a short distance farther south. The river that separates Texas from Mexico is shallow because the Texans drain off much of its water for irrigation. Where there is irrigation there are field jobs that barely pay the U.S. minimum wage in most cases but could look attractive to unemployed or underemployed Mexicans. And where there are field jobs, there are jobs in packing plants and elsewhere. Hence the large number of migrants, both legal and otherwise.

The Mexican side of the border presents, if possible, an even less appealing profile. In a bizarre sort of way, there is hope here: people from poorer regions of Mexico have at least a shot at a better economic future. But visitors should be prepared for an assault on the senses and sensibilities. The first impression when straying from the main commercial areas of a Mexican border town is one of unrelieved ugliness and gloom, and this is an impression that lasts. Almost everything looks as if it was jerry-built only yesterday and yet is already coated with multiple layers of grime.

Visitors are struck by a pervasive seediness that is not as evident deeper inside Mexico. The border seems to blend the more debased elements of the American and Mexican cultures in an unappetizing stew. A tacky commercialism brings out a barely veiled sense of frustrated envy. Something important has vanished here from Mexico's rich cultural heritage.

Tijuana, the biggest of the border towns, established its fame when Prohibition in the U.S. drove thousands of thirsty Americans to its sleazy bars and exotic nightlife. Ciudad Juárez is the next biggest and has even less appeal. "If you reach the border early enough," a leading guidebook advises travellers crossing into Ciudad Juárez from El Paso, Texas, "there is little reason not to catch a southbound bus or train immediately."[10] The same guidebook says of Nogales, across from its Arizona twin city of the same name, that it "has everything Tijuana has — curio shops (overflowing with wrought-iron bird cages, tacky felt paintings, plaster renditions of Mickey Mouse), cheap bars and plenty of liquor stores — but all on a much smaller scale."[11]

It should not be forgotten that poor people live here. They arrive in search of jobs, and often they are rewarded. Compared to poor people in more settled parts of Mexico, residents here are more likely to be newcomers and less likely to live in communities that have had time to deal with basic social and esthetic needs. When population growth outstrips the supply of adequate housing, the only immediate solution is inadequate housing, which spreads higgledy-piggledy over the hillsides and into the ravines, with large families often sharing one or two rooms. Basic amenities such as piped water, sewer lines and street lighting do arrive eventually, but only after a wait of many years. The more fortunate often prefer to move out, giving way to fresh arrivals.

An element of greed comes into play here, which may seem an unfair rap on workers whose daily wages typically amount to what an American or Canadian worker makes in an hour. It's no secret that people are lured to the border region by a chimera of abundance and by the assumption that things have to be better so close to the prosperity of the U.S. Jobs are easier to find than elsewhere in Mexico, and wages do tend to be higher, but so do living costs, especially housing and transport. Adding to an unsettled atmosphere, the border towns have long been way stations for young Mexicans trying their luck farther north. Many make several attempts before finally evading the U.S. Border Patrol.

The biggest employers now in most border towns are *maquiladoras*, in-bond assembly plants established by foreign companies, principally American but with a smattering of Japanese and others, to serve the U.S. market with low-wage labour. U.S. regulations established in 1965 have allowed goods assembled in Mexico with American components to enter the U.S. almost duty-free. Only in the last few years has this program really hit its stride, and at last count (in early 1993) there were about 2,600 factories operating under these provisions in a broad variety of industries.

Maquiladoras form only a small part of the Mexican industrial structure, but they have been a source of endless fascination to opponents of NAFTA, and it is not entirely clear why. Perhaps it is because of their export orientation and fears of a threat to jobs farther north. Or perhaps it is the horror stories about hazardous working conditions, weak enforcement of labour standards and careless disposal of toxic wastes. But these abominations are hardly unique to plants operating under the *maquiladora* system; they are common in much of Mexican industry. Eliminating *maquiladoras* would do little to eradicate abuses; something more fundamental is needed.

The fact that most *maquiladoras* are concentrated along the border speaks volumes about basic weaknesses in Mexico's economy. (This concentration has led to a common misunderstanding in Canada that

maquiladora refers to the border area itself.) Nothing in the regulations says they have to be so near the U.S. boundary. But with
Mexico's ramshackle highway, railway and telephone systems, it
makes sense to keep supply lines as short as possible — despite high
labour turnover in the border towns and lower wages elsewhere in
Mexico. Something as simple as installing a telephone can require
weeks of pleading and the payment of substantial sums. It is easier
to do long-distance phoning, and much else, from an office across
the border.

There comes a point where the *maquiladora* system begins to lose
its logic. The in-bond nature of these factories means they operate in
a closed circuit. In the absence of a free trade deal, their products
can incorporate only a minimal quantity of Mexican components and
still qualify for unrestricted entry into the U.S. And since most
components come from outside Mexico, the goods they produce
cannot be sold freely in the Mexican market. As industrialists in the
Mexican interior become more sophisticated, they will want to compete as suppliers to *maquiladoras*. And as the Mexican consumer
market grows, it will make sense to supply some of this demand from
these same factories. Future industrial development both along the
border and in the interior will be held back unless the in-bond rules
are stripped away, and this can happen only with some broader trade
agreement such as NAFTA. It should also be noted that the automobile industry, now a star export performer but long oriented to the
domestic market, has its major plants far from the border. Vehicle
assembly and manufacture of major components such as engines is
performed in cities including Puebla, Cuernavaca and Toluca in
central Mexico as well as Aguascalientes, Saltillo, Chihuahua and
Hermosillo farther north.

NAFTA does have its detractors inside Mexico, but they have not
wielded much influence. Two years before Canada's wrenching free
trade debate of 1988, Mexico went through a similar national debate
over entry into the General Agreement on Tariffs and Trade. Among
the foremost supporters of GATT entry were U.S.-trained economists
working in government ministries and the private financial sector, as
well as leaders of the more dynamic industrial sectors. Opposing
GATT entry was a motley assortment of left-wing intellectuals,
right-wing nationalists, and a lazy, pampered coterie of business
people laughably referred to as industrialists. The government, then
headed by President Miguel de la Madrid, threw its awesome propaganda machine behind GATT, and years later opponents still had not

rebuilt their morale or their arguments sufficiently to launch a coherent campaign against NAFTA.

Mexico had long followed policies of import substitution (the development of local industry to produce goods that otherwise would be imported). This helped spur sustained economic growth in the 1950s, the 1960s and into the 1970s, but these policies were kept in place long after they had outlived their usefulness. When world oil prices started rising in 1973, Mexico began to depend on oil for a hefty share of its export revenues. When prices fell just as rapidly starting in 1981, the Mexican economy remained seriously hooked on oil revenues and was left without a properly diversified export base.

Unable to cope with import bills and foreign debt payments at the same time, Mexico defaulted on its loans in 1982, causing years of financial agony both for itself and for the multitude of foreign bankers who were slow to accept responsibility for their profligate and careless lending practices. As the economy headed into a tailspin, the disgraced outgoing president, José López Portillo, nationalized the entire Mexican banking industry in a vainglorious and unsuccessful attempt to rescue his shabby image.

The 1980s were a decade of deep recession in Mexico. Living standards that had ridden the crest of the oil wave were brought brutally down to earth, and wage-earners found their purchasing power cut in half as annual inflation briefly hit triple digits. The hapless De la Madrid, elected to a six-year term in 1982, began to lay the basis for an economic recovery but saw little improvement during his time in office. His handpicked successor, Carlos Salinas de Gortari, was declared the winner in the fraud-tainted 1988 election and reinvigorated existing policies aimed at shrinking the budget deficit and opening the economy to foreign competition.

Salinas was luckier than his predecessor. Under his stewardship real growth returned to the Mexican economy, but in the eyes of his advisers something more was needed to help cement Mexico's most market-oriented set of policies since before the Revolution of the 1910s. NAFTA is Salinas's baby, and it found ready takers in both the Bush White House and its Ottawa appendage.

And so Mexico should now be set to swamp all of North America with the products of its abundant dollar-an-hour labour. Right? Well, not quite. Low wages are an advantage to exporters, but only to the extent that they can be translated into lower unit production costs. If wages were the sole determining factor, then Albania and Mali and

Laos should all be industrial powerhouses; clearly they are not. The world's most formidable trading powers, to this day, are high-wage countries such as Germany and Japan. And once the leap is made from Third World status to something approaching the First World, wages tend to rise, as Taiwan and South Korea have discovered.

Mexico faces some big obstacles. Here are a few:

(1) Labour remains plentiful but, until skill levels rise, productivity will be hampered.

(2) Capable managers are rare, and they command higher salaries than their counterparts in wealthier countries; mediocre managers are more common and achieve less impressive results — poor management means poor productivity.

(3) Mexican infrastructure needs expensive improvements, in telephones and port facilities and any number of other areas.

(4) Local capital markets have grown rapidly but are still not highly developed, making it difficult for Mexican-owned firms to raise the funds they need through share issues or local bank financing.

(5) The inflation-adjusted value of the peso rose significantly against the U.S. dollar through the early 1990s, wiping out any advantage previously conferred by an undervalued currency. (This will bring nods of recognition from Canadian exporters who suspect that the Canadian dollar was pushed artificially high in the late 1980s to ease U.S. acceptance of the original FTA.)

Now to demolish another myth. Low wages allow labour-intensive industry to thrive. Right? Well, not always. Even before NAFTA was to come into effect, Mexico had chopped away at its quota and tariff walls, providing freer entry to goods from around the world. As a result, the same "soft" sectors of the economy that have been decimated in Canada and the U.S. by competition from abroad have also suffered gravely in Mexico. Makers of textiles, apparel, footwear, toys and plastic goods have lost substantial market share to imports. Layoffs have been massive, and battered firms are in no position to launch export assaults in the U.S. or Canada. Low wages are no guarantee that jobs will survive unless quality and productivity are up to scratch.

Things will not stay like this forever. Mexico will be a more serious competitor before too long. Young people are bringing enhanced skills into the workplace, and managers are making strides in quality control, often a weak spot in Mexican industry. Some firms in the "soft" sectors will modernize and achieve comebacks, though it may be difficult.

The automotive sector, as we mentioned, is now a very robust part of the Mexican economy. Once a backwater that existed only because it could hide behind draconian regulations dictating that vehicles had to be assembled in Mexico to be sold there, the industry has come a long way. Investment in new plants has been brisk, with money pouring in from the U.S., Japan and Germany. With sturdy management and full access to the designs and worldwide marketing of their parent companies, Mexican automobile plants can take good advantage of wage differentials and build a solid export base. Trade figures over the last few years show this clearly: autos and auto parts account for a big chunk of Mexico's lopsided surplus in bilateral trade with Canada. In 1992, for instance, autos and auto parts accounted for $1.15 billion of Mexico's $2.75 billion in exports to Canada, but only $146 million of Canada's $771 million in exports to Mexico.[12]

This, of course, is not how it was supposed to be. For years free trade proponents were heard to argue that Mexicans would take the low-wage jobs in labour-intensive industries such as clothing and leave Canadians with the cream of high-paying jobs — and the automotive industry in Canada, as layoff-prone as it has been, remains a high-wage sector. But let's not forget either that this element of continental integration was in the works years before NAFTA was even a whisper; it was proceeding even without a formal trade agreement. What may change under NAFTA is not the principle of integration — this was established years ago by Detroit's Big Three — but merely its scale, as automakers from three continents decide where to deploy their future manufacturing capacity.

Fortunately for auto workers in Canada — and less fortunately for their Japanese fellows — recent changes in the world auto industry mean that job gains in Mexico are more likely to come at Japanese expense than at Canadian or U.S. expense. After years of finger-pointing and slow-footed resistance, Detroit has started getting its act together and coming up with the new designs and manufacturing techniques that will help it regain ground on its Japanese rivals. The sky-high yen is making Japan a less attractive place to export from. And NAFTA's tough North American content rules will, for a while anyway, assure Canadian and U.S. parts makers of a sizeable market in Mexican auto plants.

It seems certain in the years ahead that Canadians, knowingly or not, will be buying more Mexican-made vehicles, or vehicles containing Mexican parts. By the same token, some of the cars sold in Mexico will be from Canada. And money spent on Mexican vehicles won't just vanish; some portion of it will return to pay for other Canadian-made goods. (The short-term benefit to Canada may be less impressive than some NAFTA supporters suggest: many Canadian firms began investigating sales possibilities in Mexico only towards the end of Mexico's import boom of the early 1990s.) Even if Canada changed course and decided to slap tariffs or quotas on cars from Mexico, Canadian consumers would be hit with higher prices with no assurance that Canadian jobs would be saved.

Fear is still an important part of the picture, and this is only natural when thousands of well-paying jobs are at stake. With unemployment high in the U.S. and Canada, any southward job movement is sure to stir resentment, and Mexico becomes a handy scapegoat.

A Mexican Wish List

We do not see it as our role to attack people who are afraid of losing their jobs. We do think it is our role to point out that, with or without NAFTA, thousands of jobs will be lost but also thousands gained. There is no doubt that there will have to be adjustments away from products that are vulnerable to low-wage competition. Thus, Serge Racine, president of Sherbrooke-based Shermag Inc., which makes top-of-the-line wooden furniture at five plants in Quebec and one in New Brunswick and has thrived on exports to the United States, argues that Canadian industry as a whole should pursue an upperrange strategy: "Canada's strategy should be the same as Germany's. We should not be producing cheap goods. We should concentrate on quality products, and then we won't have as many problems. We have a culture which is better suited to quality."[13]

Given the low volume of Canada-Mexico trade and the weak state of much of Mexican industry, the early impact of NAFTA on Canada is likely to be small. And just as the Canada-U.S. free trade deal accentuated certain economic trends without being their original or only cause, so it will be with NAFTA. Blaming Mexico won't help.

One way for Canada to avoid some of the casualties of industrial change would be to retreat from the world and wallow in a sort of Brezhnevite stagnation. But this is nobody's first choice. There are other ways ahead. A more responsible attitude from government and industry than we saw during the Mulroney years would go a long way towards building and improving the job training programs the country needs to enhance work skills and assure human dignity.

Canada has some serious catching up to do here, whatever trade policies it adopts towards Mexico or any other country.

One persistent and disturbing irony of the great world trade debate is the tendency of many people who claim they favour a narrowing of the gap between rich and poor to reject some of the trade policies that could bring this goal closer to reality. In the European Community there has been strong resistance even from social democrats to lowering import barriers against Eastern European farm products, textiles and steel, precisely the areas where the Eastern countries have a competitive edge and can earn the foreign currency they need to raise their economic standards and to buy more goods from the west. Future prosperity, and lower consumer prices, are being sacrificed on the altar of short-term job preservation without looking at the many new jobs that could be created in the future.

In North America the same fears are at work. Many people have been frightened into believing that NAFTA means Canadian and U.S. workers will have to ratchet down their wages until some vague equilibrium is reached with Mexico. This was not the experience of workers in high-wage Germany when lower-wage Spain and Portugal entered the EC, and it need not happen on this side of the water. Mexico may gain more from NAFTA than Canada does, but if both sides gain something, is there not some justice in seeing the poorer partner make faster progress than the wealthier partner? Some of today's scaremongering bears an unhappy resemblance to the reactionary twaddle that early in this century warned the propertied classes of dire consequences if their social inferiors were allowed to improve their status.

We also hear NAFTA opponents mourn the dismal living and working conditions of many Mexican industrial workers. We hear rather less about how continued trade barriers can improve these conditions. Trade, for all the displacement it causes, can create opportunities for more Mexicans to find steady work. Unemployment will not vanish as if by miracle and could well rise in the early going as marginal businesses succumb, but a healthier industrial base — and, some years down the road, a stronger agricultural system — will enable workers to become fussier about the wages and working conditions they accept. If Mexican auto workers, to take a very pertinent example, sense that their employers are making excessive margins on the vehicles they export, they can push more effectively for higher wages and benefits. As we have argued, ratcheting can be an upward phenomenon as well.

Mexico's mainstream trade union movement, we hasten to add, has an unfortunate history of subservience to the perpetually ruling Institutional Revolutionary Party (known by its Spanish initials PRI), but a generational change appears imminent in the top leadership. The nonagenarian Fidel Velásquez, head of the main labour federation, can't last forever, and his demise may herald big changes. The time is ripe for Canadian and U.S. trade unionists to step up their international contacts. In a May 1993 speech marking a reconciliation of sorts between the United Auto Workers of America and the Canadian Auto Workers, UAW president Owen Bieber stated that "transnational corporations must be met with united worker power that also transcends international boundaries." That message needs to be heard more strongly, and will find a receptive audience, in Mexico as well.

One negotiating tactic that has found its way into a growing number of North American contract disputes is something known in union circles as jawboning. This involves the threat of moving production to another plant where the workforce may be readier to make concessions, and it has been used effectively to play off groups of workers against one another. Companies with plants in Mexico evidently have greater scope for jawboning and can try to ratchet down the wages of their Canadian or U.S. employees even further — if they are allowed to get away with it. But there is no need to allow this practice to become entrenched. Unions may have to work harder at building solidarity across international borders (and inside national borders, for that matter), and workers should be bolder in calling the corporate bluff. Many firms that did move production to Mexico later regretted it, finding the going tougher than they expected; several returned home, in a quiet admission of defeat. Some types of manufacturing are indeed cheaper in Mexico, but in other areas unit production costs are actually higher despite low wages. If the advantages of moving to Mexico were really substantial, companies would simply pick up and leave rather than seek penny-ante concessions from Canadian workers.

As we mentioned earlier, President Salinas has put great stock in NAFTA and hopes it can help catapult Mexico towards First World status. NAFTA is the symbolic centrepiece of his version of *perestroika*: he will do what he deems necessary to see that it is concluded. With George Bush in the White House, Salinas knew he would not be pressed to make as many concessions in matters such as labour and environmental standards, which may explain why in

1992 he appeared to neglect the ascendancy of Bill Clinton. He was paying the price for this in 1993 — with delays in congressional ratification, more appendages to the agreement than he could easily sell to nationalists at home, and a drop in capital inflows while potential investors assessed what was happening.

Although political opposition to NAFTA has been quiet in Mexico, voices have been raised both against the form the deal has taken and against the very idea of free trade. Essayist José Angel Conchello has taken the latter approach. His book *El TLC: Un callejón sin salida* (NAFTA: A Dead End) is a polemic against the excessively competitive nature of modern capitalism. His slant is fundamentally autarkist: he questions the need to strive for higher exports, urges self-sufficiency in food production, and raises concerns about who controls the economy. Foreign investment, he believes, can be replaced by self-help projects.[14]

Conchello points to difficulties posed by rules of origin when components come from varied sources, and he raises the very legitimate question of whether a trade pact that is resolutely regional in nature really paves the way to globalization. But he is inclined to nostalgic excess, and he displays his ignorance of economic reality in asserting, for instance, that love of the land has enabled Japanese farmers to become rice exporters. (In fact, rice production in Japan is hopelessly expensive, and only a ferocious political lobby keeps foreign rice from pouring in.)

We get a very different kind of argument from Jorge G. Castañeda and Carlos Heredia, two well-known academics and commentators whose article in the January 1993 issue of the Mexican magazine *Nexos* presents some original and useful ideas about what a free trade agreement should contain.[15] It is no surprise, they say, that NAFTA as it now stands has such a relentlessly neoconservative and market-obsessed bias, given that its creators — Salinas, Bush and Mulroney — were so deeply mired in neoconservative thinking. Castañeda and Heredia opt instead for what they refer to as a social democratic approach to free trade, something more along the lines of how the European Community evolved. They present seven points that they think should be included in the North American agreement:

(1) a regional development fund comparable to the EC's structural fund to help poorer regions build their economies and the skills of their workforces, with local participation in deciding how money is spent;

(2) a trilateral industrial policy, not to replace the private sector in determining winners and losers but rather to build a government-industry alliance in technological development and promotion of comparative advantages within North America;

(3) a regulatory and planning framework to establish certain fundamental guidelines;

(4) an agreement on labour mobility, a very spiny question but one that is central to economic integration (Castañeda and Heredia point out that in the previous five years some three million Mexicans living illegally in the U.S. had their status regularized through a series of amnesties; a more rational and systematic approach would seem to be in order);

(5) establishment of minimum norms in labour standards and in their enforcement;

(6) ditto for environmental standards;

(7) a dispute settlement mechanism that would be open to everyone, not just to government and industry.

Certainly there are plenty of nits to pick here. Points (1) and (4) present thornier problems than in Europe if only because the gaps, say between poorer parts of Mexico and wealthier parts of the U.S., are broader than anything within the EC. Points (2) and (3) have to be approached gingerly to avoid the creation of obstructive, tyrannical or merely wrongheaded bureaucracies. Points (5) and (6) are motherhood issues for anyone to the left of Attila the Hun; at the time of writing, the Clinton administration was pushing for something similar. And point (7), if it is taken seriously, should help make NAFTA more appealing to many doubters.

As an overall approach, these seven points have considerable merit even if they provoke some fundamental quibbles. The article in *Nexos* suggests that loss of trade rights could be dangled as a threat to ensure enforcement of certain provisions, but in practice this might be hard to do. And one glaring omission is the question of human rights, something Castañeda and Heredia have not shied away from in previous writings. Mexico's human rights record has been good when compared with the record in much of Latin America, but dismal when compared with the record in Western Europe or North America. Standards obviously have to be set higher. A trade agreement does not necessarily confer a Good Housekeeping seal of approval on every signatory's behaviour, but it is something to take into account. The EC has its Court of Human Rights, and this may be worth imitating.

This question was addressed in a 1992 speech by Ed Broadbent, former federal NDP leader and president of the Montreal-based, Ottawa-financed International Centre for Human Rights and Democratic Development:

> The trade agreement has human rights implications, whether or not the governments explicitly acknowledge this. . . . Certainly there are human rights problems in all three countries. However, despite recent signs of progress, Mexico continues to have the worst record of the three. . . . If negotiators want to encourage the mobility of capital, they must also encourage mobility of related labour rights. Canadian and American companies should have to respect basic and universally recognized rights, including the right to form a union of one's choice, in their employment practices. . . .
>
> The strongest option is to include within the body of the agreement a minimal set of key rights, which would be implemented with the same rigour as its economic provisions. A weak option, which I do not recommend, would be simply to put such rights in the preamble in the final agreement. . . . A third option would be to establish an independent monitoring agency with a mandate to examine how workers' and other rights are affected by the trilateral trade agreement. . . . The agency's findings could have considerable influence on the three governments, each of which is sensitive to domestic and international opinion on human rights.[16]

Broadbent's recommendations obviously did not carry much weight with NAFTA's original drafters, but something along these lines could be incorporated in future revisions to the deal.

As noted, NAFTA is very much a reflection of the governments that brought it into being. None of these governments is permanent. The Bush administration is gone, replaced by a new set of people who are not quite as dogmatically committed to neoconservative principles. Mulroney has stepped down, and whatever the results of the 1993 election (the campaign was in progress a the time of writing), there are bound to be changes in approach. Mexico goes to the polls in 1994, and Salinas is constitutionally barred from seeking a new term; the PRI stands an even better chance of winning than in recession-dampened 1988, but it is not certain the new president will share Salinas's pro-business mania.

NAFTA, just like European economic treaties beginning with the 1951 Treaty of Paris, is a living organism. It will evolve over time. It can grow both in scope and in membership. The shape it takes will reflect the will of the governments of the day, most particularly of the U.S. government, which will remain the dominant force if only for reasons of sheer economic might. The current crew in Washington has started off looking more *simpático* than its Republican predecessors.

One can wish that Washington did not play as dominant a role. The only way this could be the case was if NAFTA ceased to be a purely regional alignment and spread its benefits, such as they are, to a much broader grouping of countries.

Building Block or Stumbling Block?

Europe and North America are not the only parts of the world where the idea of trade blocs has emerged. In the 1960s a number of trade-promoting regional organizations were established, but scarcely any of them fulfilled their missions. These included the Central American Common Market (which was a dead letter from the start but which, for decades, has maintained a widely ignored secretariat in Guatemala City) and the Association of South-East Asian Nations (ASEAN). ASEAN was strictly a Cold War creation, instigated by U.S. fears of a domino effect in the Vietnam war. Its members are Indonesia, the Philippines, Thailand, Malaysia, Brunei and Singapore, good capitalists all. ASEAN has been more a talking shop than a serious economic or political alliance, and its original *raison d'être* is so out of date that it recently considered admitting Vietnam as an associate member.

The governments of several Asian countries have been alarmed by the walls they see going up around Europe and North America with the trade-displacing effects of the EC and NAFTA. Malaysia's long-serving prime minister, Mahathir Mohamad, has urged Japan to take the leadership in establishing an East Asian trading bloc as a defensive move.

The Japanese, shy about playing any vigorous political role, have demurred, partly because they want to avoid rekindling memories of the brutal colonial empire, dubbed the Co-Prosperity Sphere, that they forged across Southeast Asia, Korea and much of China before and during the Second World War. A more important reason may be

Washington's explicit disapproval of such a move and Japan's obvious interest in avoiding any further exacerbation of trade tensions between the two countries.

But perhaps the crowning reason is that the Japanese don't talk about building tight economic alliances — they simply go out and do it. The economic power wielded by Japanese-based multinational companies across much of Eastern Asia is such that any formal, politically inspired alliance might seem superfluous. An unofficial Co-Prosperity Sphere is up and running, kindled by economic rather than military might and leaving new factories rather than defeated armies in its wake.

Regionalism in trade matters has resurfaced in other parts of the world as well. Mexico has a bilateral trade agreement with Chile that predates NAFTA and at the time of writing was negotiating a trilateral agreement with Colombia and Venezuela. Farther south, Brazil, Argentina, Uruguay and Paraguay were preparing to set up the *Mercosur* (Southern Market) to encourage regional integration (while Chile, distressed by Brazil's fiscal indiscipline, decided to stay out). In eastern and southern Africa there have been murmurings of regional trade bodies. And the U.S. had signed a bilateral deal with Israel well before it talked free trade with Canada. At least under George Bush, the U.S. promoted the idea of a trade grouping extending from Alaska to Tierra del Fuego in keeping with his "Enterprise for the Americas" approach.

But not everyone agrees with the wisdom of a regional approach to trade. This is a subject of keen debate among economists, many of whom feel the GATT, with its mandate to set rules that favour worldwide trade, offers a more hopeful approach. Most economists insist that trade is a good thing and that, as a general rule, it enhances economic well being. Hence, measures to remove obstacles to trade should be welcomed. One reason the appointment of Laura Tyson as head of President Clinton's Council of Economic Advisers raised some eyebrows is that she is among those relatively few economists who do not instinctively favour freer trade.

Some defenders of regionalism argue that regional trade groupings are a building block rather than a stumbling block in the erection of worldwide free trade. They may point out that GATT rules do, after all, make specific provision for regional groupings. They may assert that regional bodies are faster and nimbler than the slow-footed multilateral approach and that the various GATT rounds seem to drag on *ad infinitum* with little to show for their efforts. But regional bodies also have been known to advance at something less than the speed of light. It took the EC more than thirty-five years from its creation to achieve an unobstructed internal market.

Critics of regionalism decry what they see as a discriminatory approach that tends to be trade-displacing rather than trade-creating. For example, a Mexican factory that imports electronic components from Taiwan may find under NAFTA that tariffs have fallen on similar components from the U.S. but not on the Taiwanese product that it initially chose because of quality or price. Accordingly, the factory may find it cheaper to shift future orders to a U.S. supplier. Thus the Taiwanese producer loses out to a less efficient U.S. competitor because of this distortion, and no new trade is created. It becomes easier now to understand Asian concerns. It may be an exaggeration to speak, as some have done, of Fortress Europe or Fortress North America, but most economic wisdom suggests that tariff structures favouring some countries over others will not deliver the full benefit that trade can provide.

Jagdish Bhagwati, professor of economics and political science at Columbia University in New York and a prolific writer on trade issues, has argued long and hard in favour of a multilateral approach. In his conclusion to a 1992 discussion paper on this topic, he makes the following observations:

U.S. regionalism, when presided over by Ambassador William Brock [United States Trade Representative in Ronald Reagan's first administration], was *not* geographically circumscribed regionalism. Rather, it was truly open-ended. Brock was known to have offered an FTA to Egypt (along with the one to Israel) and to the ASEAN countries; indeed, he would have offered it to the moon and Mars if only life had been discovered there with a government in place to negotiate with. . . .

By contrast, today's regionalism, confined to the Americas by President Bush's men, lacks the "vision thing". In fact, when allied with Secretary [of State James] Baker's recently reported admonition to the Japanese not to encourage an Asian trade bloc, as suggested by Malaysia as a necessary response to the EC and U.S. regionalism, the U.S. policy appears to Asia also to be self-contradictory and self-serving: "regional blocs are good for us but not for you." And it simply won't wash, though Japan, fearing further bashing, will be deterred for a while.[17]

In the early months of the Clinton administration, it was difficult to tell which way Washington was leaning — whether it favoured a regional, a multilateral or simply a stand-pat position. But it certainly was receiving plenty of advice. Despite his misgivings about how regionalism might affect the evolution of world trade, Bhagwati does manage to come up with an optimistic scenario:

> If America's regionalism is not to turn into a piecemeal, world-trading-system-fragmenting force, it is necessary to give it a programmatic, world-trade-system-unifying format and agenda. One possibility is to encourage, not discourage, Japan to line up the Asian countries (all the way to the Indian sub-continent) into an AFTA [Asian Free Trade Agreement], with the U.S. lining up the South Americans into the NAFTA, on a schedule of, say, ten years. Then Japan and the U.S., the two "hubs", would meet and coagulate into a larger FTA at that point, finally negotiating with the EC and its associate countries to arrive at the grand finale of multilateral free trade for all in Geneva.[18]

How plausible is all this, and where might it leave Canada? In the next chapter, we will argue that the development of regional trading blocs is more likely to impede global free trade than advance it. But however global free trade is achieved, it will serve Canadian interests — and not just business interests — more promisingly than staying in a regionalist rut or rejecting free trade entirely. We are puzzled by assertions to the effect that a country that opens its borders to world trade is somehow diminished. We don't particularly like the text of NAFTA or the people who signed it, but it does enhance trade possibilities with a neglected southern partner and to say no would be a slap in the face to the idea of broadened trade. It would be more useful to work towards making NAFTA less socially regressive and less restrictive than simply to reject it.

We would also rather see a faster transition to a multilateral approach. One problem with the original Canada-U.S. FTA and now with NAFTA is that it ties Canada too closely to its most natural trading partner. Let us explain. For reasons of geography, it is obvious the U.S. will continue to account for a predominant share of Canada's international trade, come what may. We are aware of the failure of Pierre Trudeau's attempted trade-diversifying Third Option (the First Option was further integration into the American economy;

the Second was the status quo). But we are wary not of this predominance in itself, which is natural and necessary, but of the way it continues to grow, impelled artificially by the trade-displacing nature of regionalism. And we are wary also of the risk that Canada could become so tightly integrated a part of the U.S. economy that this could hamper future attempts to build independent ties with other trading partners.

In the next chapter, we will argue that Canada should break away from the current regionalist approach (if the U.S. doesn't do so first) and seek free trade agreements with whomever will agree to go along. It could be with Japan or Australia or Cameroon (though not likely with Mars). It could even be with the EC once it gets some of its conundrums sorted out. Canada and its friends should also be pushing vigorously for an acceleration of multilateral GATT talks. If Canada loses patience with the pace of GATT, or if Washington gets caught up in one of its periodic tantrums with an overseas trading partner, then Canada should plough ahead on its own rather than get dragged behind.

Chapter 5

One World or Three?

We have seen that while the need for a public authority to organize and oversee economic affairs has not diminished, the capacity of the existing system of nation-states to perform that function is under increasing challenge. One response to that challenge has been a move towards the formation of larger economic units, and it is this move that has given rise to much of the brave talk about globalization. But a global economy, or even the more limited development of a global free trade system, is not the only possible outcome of the move towards larger units. An equally logical and, in the light of history, perhaps more likely eventuality is the division of the world into mutually hostile trading blocs. We looked at the internal structure of these trading blocs in chapter four. In this chapter we turn to the relations among the major blocs, examine the impact of the end of the Cold War and the emerging economic strategy of the United States, and see what possibilities exist for Canada to retain some room for manoeuvre as new structures take shape.

Competition and Globalism

In the wake of the defeat of Communism and the end of the Cold War with all its menacing implications, it is sometimes difficult to remember that the wars of our century have been fought not between competing social systems on ideological grounds but between capitalist states competing for markets, trade and economic advantage. Substitute trading blocs for empires, and the "new world order" as it is being defined seems remarkably like the old world disorder before the Bolshevik interlude. Indeed, if anything it appears even more unstable and dangerous.

"Peace is wonderful. I like it as much as the next man," wrote University of Chicago political scientist John J. Mearsheimer in a prophetic essay entitled "Why We Will Soon Miss the Cold War."[1] However, he continues, "we are likely soon to regret the passing of the Cold War." Mearsheimer makes it clear that he is not a reconstructed cold warrior. He does not want to revisit the war in Korea or Vietnam or the "domestic Cold War." He says that "we will not wake up one day to discover fresh wisdom in the collected fulminations of John Foster Dulles." But in the absence of the discipline of the Cold War, a political anarchy develops that cannot be contained within concepts of interdependence. The end of the Cold War ended a period of relative economic and political stability, particularly in Europe.

One expression of the new instability is the rather contradictory concept of "competition within the global economy." This competition is supposed to take place between the emerging trading blocs, which replace individual nation-states as market entities. But competition within the blocs, among the various national components, continues or even becomes more intense, as illustrated by the controversial movement of the Hoover plant from France to Scotland (see chapter four) and the increase in the number, variety and bitterness of disputes between Canada and the United States. Interbloc trade — international trade — becomes even more problematic as the blocs, as they are becoming constituted, are universal and self-contained. The issue is thus how to protect the internal market and make inroads into the other's market.

Trade was once fundamentally an exchange of different goods or services. As *The Economist* so lyrically put it, "In the days when clippers raced across the oceans, the point of trade was a clear as the ships were beautiful. They sailed to Japan or China or Australia loaded with something that Britain had and the Japanese wanted and returned with tea, silk or wool."[2] But the old days of mercantile capitalism are gone with the clipper ships. In our brave new world of "the big bang," round-the-clock markets and the effortless flow of currency through the ionosphere, everyone has the same thing to sell.

Still, there is something strange about a global economy that seeks a balance in the mutual purchase of each other's automobiles. If two or more partners produce the same things, trade is affected only by the relative advantage of one producer over the other. Competition is a zero-sum game. It used to be described as carrying coals to Newcastle. Nonetheless, Reuter carried a report of a speech by U.S. trade representative Mickey Kantor to the American Semiconductor Industry Association in which he claimed to be "resolute and determined" to make sure Japan buys more U.S. computer chips. Under a 1990 agreement, Japan was supposed to buy 20 per cent of its computer chips from the U.S. and now only purchases 15.9 per cent — not good enough in Mr. Kantor's eyes.[3] Well, it's not quite the equivalent of Admiral Perry steaming into Tokyo harbour. Moreover, for every reported threat to Japan, an example of American-Japanese joint ventures or economic cooperation can be cited — all of which points to the complexity of the current economic process. But the concept of competition makes a very nervous fit with globalism, in which the sounds of a trade war are often discernible.

Thus the new global order becomes remarkably like the old global order. And in the old global order, there has always been Act Two. Someone rises in a country like Germany and demands "Lebensraum." Or another country in Asia, perhaps, decides to challenge Anglo-European domination and creates an Asian Co-Prosperity Zone. And it doesn't have to occur on what have been traditional fault lines. Russia, on its knees or perhaps even on its back, can still demand suzerainty over its traditional Asian empire. And that may just be for starters.

Hegemony, not competition, characterizes a global economy — hegemony, however fragile or temporary it may be, by one or another economic power. Thus, the concept of trading blocs within a single global economic system is a contradiction in terms and where it exists, as it does now, it is essentially unstable. In the past, the resolution has been war. If war is excluded — a notion that may be more wishful than strategic thinking — there must be some other resolution to the competition. It is in this area that there is validity in the various expressions of modern globalism.

The old global economy was relatively stable when it excluded blocs. The American economy was made powerful by a number of factors, including population base, resources and all the other attributes that Karl Marx described as the conditions providing for the uneven development of capitalist economies. This process, rapidly accelerated by the First and Second World Wars, created a New Global Economy, which replaced the Old Global Economy represented by Britain, which in turn replaced an even older global economy that (if one excludes the overland caravans of antiquity) is the economic expression of the post-Columbian world.

Walter Russell Mead, author of *Mortal Splendor: The American Empire in Transition*, envisions

a world made up of three rival blocs: one based in the Western European nations; one dominated by Japan; and the American bloc. The third major bloc is the weakest and most troubled. It is, unfortunately, ours. America's protectionists and neo-isolationists seem to think that a protected Pan-American bloc could strengthen the U.S. economy, but they are sadly mistaken. There aren't enough customers in it. Economically, the United States and Canada are too much like twins to grow rich trading largely with each other. Latin America is in a prolonged economic decline. From 1981 to 1987, to cite just one figure, imports to Argentina, Mexico and Brazil — the three largest economies in Latin America — fell 36 per cent. . . . Moreover, Latin America does not seem eager to tie its future to the United States. The president of Mexico went to Harvard, his children attend a Japanese school in Mexico City. . . . In a world of rival blocs, the Asian and European blocs are almost certain to be more appealing to the Latin Americans than one dominated by gringos; our bloc, along with all its other weaknesses, will be full of defectors and aspiring defectors.

We will put aside for the moment the question of whether it is too soon or too late to put Canada among the "aspiring defectors" and note that Mead considers the European bloc the most coherent and stable of the three. As he points out, division and specialization within Europe will mean that they will have "very little need of or interest in goods or services from Asia or the Americas."[4]

In a speech in Toronto early in 1993, American economist Lester Thurow presented a list prepared by the Japanese of the seven industries they want to dominate by the twenty-first century: science industries, telecommunications, civil aviation, machine tools, robots, computers and software. He also claimed to have seen a list prepared by the Germans containing exactly the same seven industrial priorities. "We don't make these lists in the United States but if we did," he added, "what do you think we would find? Exactly the same seven industries."[5] We suggest you would find those seven and a few others: steel, auto, vacuum cleaners, nuts and bolts and every widget known to the industrial age. That is what President Clinton, his academic gurus and trade negotiators are doing. They call it "strategic trade."

The context is that of the 1990s, the first decade since the end of the Second World War in which the world economy has not grown. Lester Thurow described Clinton's problem as "how to get the American economy to grow in a world that isn't growing."[6] This is a new and perhaps more useful way of looking at the central issue in an economic and historical debate that has been raging in the United States for a number of years. On one side is a whole school of American economic and historical thought called the "declinists" whose devotees have written some of the current period's most interesting literature — fiction and nonfiction. They have now been joined by a new school of, shall we suggest, "non-declinists," whose central thesis is that however bad it may be in the U.S., it is worse everywhere else. Consider, for example, George Will:

> The modern presidency, devoted to incessant manipulation of public opinion, manufactures ersatz crises to hold public attention. Hence Clinton's overheated rhetoric about America's "decline."

> Japan's economy is reeling, Germany's growth rate has lagged behind America's since the 1970s and its GNP is shrinking. Both Britain and France have double-digit unemployment.[7]

The "non-declinists" are an adjunct to, possibly a subsection of, the "triumphalists" who take their cue from the end of, and the apparent American victory in, the recently terminated Cold War, as well as the brief assertion of American power in the even more recent hot war in the Persian Gulf.

The Unipolarity Bubble

The Gulf War seemed to confirm the military primacy of the United States. For a brief period, the might of the U.S. was once again indisputable. Ah, the heady days of the "New World Order." What an era those few short months were!

The New World Order was in part an outgrowth of the events of 1989, which even before it was over was proclaimed as the most important year in history. With the exception of a few unrepentant old-line Communists, there was something for everyone in 1989. For those who enjoy the symmetry of anniversaries, 1989 was compared to 1789, the year of the French Revolution. (The Thermidorian Reaction appears, however, to be running ahead of schedule.) A self-confessed Hegelian, Francis Fukuyama, emerged from somewhere in the bowels of the U.S. State Department to write "The End of History" in which he rescued Hegel's original notion of the dialectical process from Karl Marx.[8] Hegel saw the dialectic leading to some future perfect spiritual union as the end of history. Marx argued that history would end in a Communist utopia. Fukuyama decided the end had come with the now obvious universal triumph of Western liberal democracy. Hegel, who seemed quite happy to live and work in pre-Bismarck Prussia, would probably have had little time for either vision.

Happily, "endism" soon reached its own. But not "triumphalism," which just got going as the Soviet Empire began to collapse. It took the events of 1991 — the Gulf War and the Soviet coup (attempted or successful, depending upon how one looks at such things) — for this notion really to gain currency. Writing in *Foreign Affairs*, Washington *Post* columnist Charles Krauthammer wrote that the post-Cold War world's most striking feature was its "unipolarity":

> In perhaps another generation or so there will be great powers coequal with the United States, and the world will, in structure, resemble the pre-World War I era. But we are not there yet, nor will we be for decades. Now is the unipolar moment.[9]

Krauthammer continued:

> There is a sharp distinction to be drawn between real and apparent multilateralism. True multilateralism involves a genuine coalition of coequal partners of comparable strength and stature — the World War II Big Three coalition, for example. What we have today is pseudo-multilateralism: a dominant great power acts essentially alone, but embarrassed at the idea and still worshipping at the shrine of collective security, recruits a ship here, a brigade there, and blessings all around to give its unilateral actions a multilateral sheen. The gulf is no more a collective operation than was Korea, still the classic case study in pseudo-multilateralism.

Krauthammer's comparison between the Gulf and Korea expresses the essential problem with his argument. In 1950, the Cold War was at its bipolar height. If one is restricted to considering the Western alliance as the universe, then this universe was, of course, unipolar (the whole concept of unipolarity is troubling — one pole suggests an opposite). But even within the confines of relative military strength and the narrowing of the universe to include only the West and its periphery, the power relationship has been altered. The U.S.

still represents the most powerful military. But this power or potential power is conditional in that several states — and with nuclear proliferation this number will increase — have the military strength, should it come to that, to inflict unacceptable costs, including annihilation, on the others. One should not push this idea too far. It is one thing to have nuclear capability and quite another to be able to deliver it. The United States is now alone in its global reach. Nevertheless, even the United States must pick its enemies with increasing care.

But military might is only one aspect of global power. As Paul Kennedy pointed out in *The Rise and Fall of the Great Powers,* military might, with its costs and demands, serves to weaken and undermine the economic strength of the imperial power — especially as its grasp declines faster than its reach, as was so clearly evident in the Persian Gulf.[10] Even in this instance, however, while it appears evident that the costs borne by the United States to expand its military have weakened and perhaps even fatally undermined its empire, there is no military challenger looming. There is no external military threat to the U.S., nor do the colonies seem to be restless.

Moreover, the Clinton administration is betting the farm that the military can be successfully cut, that the economy can be adjusted, and that there is such a thing as a "peace dividend" that can be channelled into the domestic economy, which can thus be made to grow enough to ward off any economic threat to its prosperity and security. This internal prosperity will be the base of the outward reach of a revitalized America, and whammo! — it's the 1940s again. But even assuming that things work out at home, all this is for the future. In the here and now, America must reassert itself and put the hammer to its trading partners to force them to cut interest rates, reduce their trade surpluses and in effect pay for the American renaissance. At least that is the way the revised script on America's future is supposed to unfold. One should notice that this script excludes both borderless and unipolar visions of the brave new world.

The "unipolar" world is a delusion. What is increasingly at issue is how strong America is in relation to the Europeans and the Japanese. The Gulf War pointed to the essential military strength of the U.S. Thus the Vietnam War represented, in baseball terms, merely one lousy season, and (if we continue the sports analogy) the Gulf vindicated the traditional loser's defiance — "wait till next year." Or as George Bush exclaimed, it put an end to the "Vietnam syndrome." But the war also expressed the weakness of the U.S. vis-à-vis its putative allies in that it chose to seek financial aid to keep its army in the field. While it may not have a direct bearing on the health of the new economic recovery, there was a sharp fall in American balance of payments figures in the early months of 1993, due in large measure to the end of foreign payments for the war in the Gulf.

There is a big difference between being the world's policeman and being a hired gun. Even if American action in the Gulf was motivated by self-interest in protecting a vital resource, it would still have been more difficult to wage this war without the approval of Europe. The world's only military superpower is constrained in a manner that no military power has been hitherto. Thus, even in the strictest and narrowest of terms, military force alone is impotent. Apart from the lesson of Vietnam, ignored by the Soviets in Afghanistan, the totality of the Soviet postwar military experience is an illustration of the impotence of military might when isolated from the actual social and economic condition of the state whose interests it defends. All this is made most vivid with pictures of the conquering army of occupation rummaging through garbage cans in Germany.

America First

So America should perhaps pause, reflect and enjoy the memories of the victory parades. They will probably be the last ones for a very long time. And as we await the memoirs, we can speculate about how much former president George Bush was taken in by the "triumphalists" when they proclaimed him President of the World. No doubt their vision corresponded at least in part to Bush's view of himself. He was The Leader of the world's leading power. In the last desperate days of the election campaign, he begged the American voters to consider the best president for an international crisis. Receiving no response, he proclaimed that his dog knew more about foreign policy than either Clinton or Gore. Neither man nor beast commented. The message the American people were about to deliver was telegraphed well ahead. They wanted a new president who would do as presidents traditionally have done: promote American economic interests — not in Europe or Asia or Latin America, where American investors have been doing very well either through the foreign operations of multinationals or in the international pool of investment capital, but in the heartland of the United States, where Americans and the American economy have been hurting. They were drawing a distinction, perhaps for the first time since the heady days of the New Deal, between the interests of American capital and those of the American people.

The message the voters were about to deliver was telegraphed by the Ross Perot phenomenon, by factory floor rallies, and by the television bites of platforms crowded with members of the business elite that began to dominate the later stages of the Clinton campaign. That ultimately successful campaign contained an aggressive message to the world articulated around such phrases as "America's projection of strength abroad must be based upon its economic power at home." There was also a message for Canada: American internationalism was about to be redefined, and the political and economic equation was about to change.

At the centre of the redefinition of America's power is the challenge to force American economic growth in a world economy that is not growing. In this economic climate — a climate that puts pressure on all partnerships and alliances — the United States faces the same problems faced by the individual countries of Europe, by Japan and the "tigers," and indeed by every national economy. It is the zero-sum game heading into the stretch. A winner and thus also losers are going to be declared. This redefinition is expressed by American trade negotiators who announce they are prepared to walk away from any and all sacred cows of the "new global economy" if American interests are not served. The issues range from immense telecommunications systems in Europe to aeronautics and semiconductors in Asia to the tax on beer cans in Ontario.

As of mid-1993, nobody really had a fix on U.S. international trade policy, but it was becoming clearer that the old rules were being changed. Thus, the Americans would criticize the Japanese for dragging their feet on the GATT and suggest they were acting as if a successful outcome of the semimoribund six years of negotiations was not important. Then, the very next morning, trade representative Mickey Kantor would say that "there are consequences of not having a successful Uruguay Round [but] they're not devastating."[11] While the Japanese quietly dismissed Kantor as new and inexperienced, the Europeans openly fretted about a trade war. One prominent German banker noted that in just two months of power the Clinton administration had announced punitive tariffs on steel, questioned the accord on subsidies to the Airbus consortium and threatened to retaliate against any real or even perceived European exclusionary practice. While exclusion is the essence of all trade blocs to some degree, and is thus to some degree universally accepted, the challenge to European procurement policies is probably the most significant step in that it is consistent with the seemingly new policy of unilateral action to force open markets wherever, whenever and however it is to the economic advantage of the United States.

The new American approach of feigned indifference to multilateral processes has even aroused fear in Latin America. Where the extension of NAFTA once seemed to be a foregone conclusion and a fast route to industrialization, it is now being seen in its political and ideological dimension. In a few short years, Mexico has been Canadianized: that is, it is being sucked into the American domestic market.

If promises by Jean Chrétien to renegotiate the Free Trade Agreement and by Audrey McLaughlin to renounce the whole project sounded somewhat silly, it is because they were and are. When these threats come from Mickey Kantor and the U.S. Congress they may be just as silly and even wrongheaded, but in this case they are quite serious. American attitudes to GATT have brought economists such as Sylvia Ostry to believe that a breakdown in the world trading system is imminent (she also blames the French). After such a breakdown "the United States would act unilaterally ... especially with its weaker partners," writes Toronto *Star* economics editor David Crane.[12] Crane goes on to suggest that GATT provides rules that must be followed by all members, and says the current FTA "provides only modest protection against U.S. actions." This is a wild overstatement. When it comes to economic dealings with Canada and Mexico, the U.S. can do just about anything it wants, when it wants. As it has demonstrated time and time again, the United States has relinquished little of its sovereignty, little of its ability to act unilaterally on any economic issue wherever and whenever it wishes. The notion of limitations on sovereignty is for other countries.

The new American administration is intent on developing a new America First economic, industrial and trade system based on a government-led strategy. The outlines are now becoming evident and the coherence of the strategy is being debated in Washington. But the simple truth is that the old order made safe by the 1944 Bretton Woods agreement began to crumble twenty-five years ago and no credible alternative has been found.

The lack of an alternative can be illustrated by the immobility of the General Agreement on Tariffs and Trade. Originally an expression of American hegemony and the natural, normal and historical demands by the dominant power for free trade, GATT has latterly turned into a forum to redress the postwar imbalance of economic power — or, if you will, the postwar unipolarity. It has, in effect, become its opposite. It thus spins its wheels because on the one hand no one country or bloc can impose its will, and on the other no one country or bloc can afford to see the process of finding a new regime that can attempt to bring order into the world trading system reach a dead end.

The fact that the United States is quickest with the ultimatums and appears the readiest to see GATT collapse may be either an expression of its residual strength — especially now that the bubble in Japan may have broken and the German economic engine is sputtering — or a mere delusion of power. In any case, the Americans have long complained about GATT. "GATT's 1940s-era assumptions," write American trade experts Clyde V. Prestowitz, Jr., Alan Tonelson and Robert W. Jerone, "have become largely irrelevant to the world economy of the 1990s — and to America's interests in that economy."[13] They continue:

> Geopolitics led the United States to open its market regardless of other countries' trade practices. Determined to contain communism by creating a stable and prosperous free-world camp and by underwriting Third World economic development and political stability, Washington encouraged its European allies to form a restrictive trade bloc, tolerated flagrant protectionism by Japan, and routinely wooed developing countries with lucrative trade concessions.

GATT is dead, or dying, in the minds of these authors and in the opinion of a growing body of experts, because the U.S. can no longer sustain it. Moreover, with the Cold War over, the U.S. doesn't have to sustain it. It was one thing to conceive of a free trade world in the 1950s when the U.S. was essentially the only big trader. It also made sense politically for the U.S. to foster economic policies that would rebuild and strengthen its putative allies in the Cold War. This was especially the case in Germany but it also operated very much in Japan. As noted earlier, this strategy contributed significantly to the growth of the powers that now represent the greatest threat to the United States.

This is not to suggest that the Uruguay Round cannot continue to be negotiated for another eight years. More likely, at some point soon a compromise will be reached which will probably have the same effect as the previous compromise of the Tokyo Round — it will keep the process alive. The Tokyo Round was essentially the first negotiation that moved beyond the issues of tariff cutbacks into more problematic areas of subsidies and harmonization of social and industrial policies. Agreements reached in aircraft development and purchases appeared to give some comfort to the Americans but were honoured mainly in the breach.

Even the most skeptical of trade economists believe the process is worthwhile — negotiation as a substitute for action is a legitimate endeavour, especially when any action could set off the ultimate catastrophic trade war. Even the most ardent "America Firsters", "protectionists" or whatever (strangely there are no nationalists in the most nationalist country in the world) do not want a complete rupture of the GATT process. Most see some advantages for the U.S. in the process, if only in using the process itself as a substitute for agreement, because the American economy and therefore American power appear to face a challenge on two fronts if not three. A prominent American trade expert, Murray Weidenbaum, writes:

> In private conversations the Europeans tell U.S. companies not to worry, that their trade restrictions, such as reciprocity and domestic content rules, are aimed at Japan. It is, however, far more than a mere riposte for the United States to say that it does not know how good their aim is. The same restrictions that adversely affect Japan can keep out U.S. goods. This may especially be the case with automobile "transplants" which are built in the United States by Japanese owned companies. Moreover, if the products of the Asian rim countries are kept out of Europe, the Western Hemisphere is their major alternative market.[14]

The third front is created by the circumstance that the traditional export of capital by the United States and more recently Japan has created some multinational companies whose nationality is hard to define. Commentators like George Will have complained that some recent American protectionist moves, such as the reclassification of various vans and recreational vehicles as trucks (thus putting them in a higher tariff category) to benefit the Chrysler Corporation, discriminate against hundreds of thousands of Americans who are employed in the manufacturing and sales of Japanese cars simply to protect a few thousand Canadians employed by Chrysler. This third front goes beyond the organization of joint ventures and relationship enterprises to permanent equity holdings. The Japanese have invested heavily in American communications and entertainment corporations such as Time Warner, and the U.S. is involved in the Japanese automotive and electronic industries. U.S. multinationals are also prominent in the EC.

Losing Control

Meanwhile, there are other conceptual problems with the global economy. For instance, is it truly global? In the old days of imperialism, and the mercantile capitalism that fostered it, all parts of the globe were brought into the economy. This is not the case today. In a large and growing part of the world — Africa, much of Latin America, the peripheries of the old British, French, Turkish and Russian empires, and perhaps even Russia itself — there is, it seems, no economy, global or otherwise. However weak and unstable, the former Communist system, which included a Communist trading bloc (Comecon), provided a mechanism as well as an opportunity for gradual integration within the European trading system, which since the 1970s and the abatement of the Cold War in Europe had been developing with increasing vigour. While in the long run Russia and Eastern Europe may serve as markets for Western countries, for now the Soviet empire appears to have collapsed too soon and too precipitously for Europe to tolerate or to adjust. The political and economic premise of the European Community included a separate Europe in the central and eastern part of the continent, making the whole much like the Europe that existed at the turn of the century. Mikhail Gorbachev lobbed two blows against the West. He deprived the Americans of an enemy and the Europeans of a market.

The geography of the "Third World" has another aspect as well, existing within the body of the most advanced industrial states. Growing areas, both rural and urban, of the United States, Britain and Canada have the statistics one associates with the Third World. This Third World grows as economic power is concentrated in fewer and fewer countries and in smaller and smaller regions even in the richest of countries. It grows also as governments in industrialized countries either lack the capacity or renounce their responsibility to provide a decent standard of living for all their citizens and the new global economy begins to resemble Hobbes's "war of all against all." One has only to consider the increasing number of impoverished regions in Canada to wonder what the real economic prospects are in that economy.

Other conceptual problems arise with the notion of interdependence. Politically, the theory goes something like this: interdependence begets cooperation, which creates growth and prosperity, which in turn increases interdependence, and so it goes. All this, of course, must be organized: thus the various national units evolve into a superstate. The problem with this theory is that the free market requires competition, and one cannot compete and cooperate at the same time. Interdependence is more likely to lead to conflict than to cooperation. If history is any guide, autarky — not dependence — is the goal of the modern state. Both the justification and the reasons for German, Japanese and even Italian actions in the years leading up to the Second World War involved autarky. The Japanese in particular feared then, just as they reject now, American efforts to interfere with and to determine Japanese trade. Interdependence is a matter not only of supplies and resources but also of trade. In this respect the United States has a huge advantage with its domestic market of 250 million people.

It is an advantage that the Europeans seek to mitigate with the creation of their own sphere. But the issue is much different when looking at the U.S. vis-à-vis Japan. Both the Americans and the Japanese consider the Pacific as one. The Japanese goal is not to establish a United States of Asia but to integrate itself into the American market. Thus the Japanese express a far different attitude towards NAFTA from that of the Europeans. And the Americans, for whom considering the Pacific as an American lake is an attribute of Manifest Destiny (see chapter two), see investment and trade in Europe in a markedly different way from investment and trade in Japan.

Control of the Pacific and the countries that border on it is as central to American policy today as it ever was. The fact that America is losing control, perhaps permanently, is at the root of the current bashing of the Japanese. American frustration is compounded by the fact that world trade has shifted to the Pacific — not only to Japan but also to the other economic "tigers" such as Taiwan, whose central bank now has foreign exchange reserves of $100 billion. Twenty million people with the largest pool of foreign exchange of any country anywhere have been negotiating to buy 40 per cent of McDonnell-Douglas's commercial aircraft business and move much of its production to the island. South Korea, Singapore and Hong Kong are also becoming economic and commercial powerhouses as well as significant markets.

One indication of the American mood has been the popularity of Michael Crichton's novel *Rising Sun*, now a major motion picture. Revolving around an alleged Japanese conspiracy to take over the American economy, the book contains snatches of dialogue and descriptions that are absolutely astounding in their blatant racism and ignorant stereotyping. Nevertheless, *Rising Sun* not only rocketed to the top of the bestseller list in 1992 but was also taken seriously by many reviewers. By appending a bibliography of nonfiction on the subject of Japan and Japanese-American relations, Crichton linked his novel with the Japan-bashing growth industry in American publishing. Many of the works that have appeared have rather apocalyptic titles: *The Coming War with Japan; The Japanese Power Game; The Silent War; Trade Wars; Zaibatsu America: How Japanese Firms Are Colonizing Vital U.S. Industries.*

The increasing racism and jingoism come in part from real or imagined pressures on the American economy and the denial of American world hegemony. Japan-bashing and assorted racist ravings are not the exclusive property of the lunatic fringe of the Republican Party. The ideas expressed by Klansman David Duke are vulgar and inane, but they are not substantially different from the ones expressed by George Bush, Bill Clinton, or for that matter Lee Iacocca and other captains of industry. The demands for national unity in the U.S. in the face of a new enemy—really a very old enemy that has confounded American goals in the Pacific since the days of Teddy Roosevelt and his adventures in the Philippines—have an ominous ring.

American paranoia is both fabled and almost all-encompassing. It can be turned with ease on an Iranian mullah or a ragtag band of revolutionaries from an impoverished country. A crazed drug dealer can be instantly turned from a CIA "asset" into a diabolical menace. In economics the Americans have been threatened by Arab oil merchants, the German economic miracle, the European common market. One does not even have to look very long through library stacks to find volumes on the potential menace of the Soviet economic miracle.

If the U.S. looks on its control of the Pacific as vital to its national security as well as its ambitions, the nations of the Pacific, especially Japan, are equally determined not to let this happen. We know our history of the war: the doomed defence of Hong Kong and the sneak attack on Pearl Harbor. (The notion that military secrets of both attack and defence are vital is of course a commonplace. It is generally considered a virtue to be able to organize and mount an attack without the enemy's knowledge.) Pearl Harbor is the "day of infamy" in Western minds. In Japan, Pearl Harbor was a preemptive strike by a weaker country against the offensive capabilities of the giant sea power that was setting out to strangle it by blockading its sources of both food and raw materials. Japan thus also remembers its prewar vulnerabilities and insists they will never emerge again.

Sensing American hostility in the current negotiations among Canada, Mexico and the U.S., which seem designed to freeze Japan out of the new American common market, the Japanese are creating a Pacific Rim trading bloc of their own which will be based upon the yen. This move, if it ever comes to fruition, will put enormous pressure on Fortress North America by freezing it out of Asia. This is one of the sources of the instability of the American bloc noted by Walter Russell Mead.

In relative decline, the U.S. is still the most powerful economy in the world and without doubt the greatest military power, but the process of change appears to be irreversible. Paul Kennedy noted the speed with which the U.S. went from being the world's banker to being the world's major debtor and the speed with which Japan rose to become the financier. Richard J. Barnet, one of the U.S.'s top foreign and economic policy experts, describes the situation in these terms: "The United States, the world's largest debtor nation, is unable to meet its payroll without the eighty billion dollars or more a year from non-American financiers it has come to depend upon."[15] A good part of this $80 billion must come from Japan. The U.S. is the supplicant. Perhaps this notion is too horrid to comprehend and Japan-bashing is merely the denial phase of a terminally ill economy.

The U.S. is as much a victim of the Cold War as Russia and thus faces a similar reappraisal of its role and future. It can turn inward and lash out at its enemies and their perfidy, a course rationalized (if racism can ever be rational) and justified in much of the literature. In Kurt Vonnegut's latest, *Hocus Pocus*, the Japanese have even taken over and operate the only growth area of the American economy, the prison system. If America is really to be involved in a trade war with Japan, will the war end with harsh words and limited economic tit for tat, or will it expand and deepen? History speaks to the latter conclusion.

Canada or USCAN?

During these arguments Canada, one assumes by some prior agreement, effectively drops off the face of the globe. It is hard not to find this unnerving, despite previous assurances that as the world moves inevitably to the one global market Canada's fate is irrelevant, even to Canadians. The Americans consider, as do most others, that Canada is henceforth an inextricable part of continental America, as a not unsubstantial market but more significantly as an energy and resource hinterland. Thus, while it still may be factually premature and certainly politically incorrect to refer to Canada and the U.S. as an integrated whole when considering internal continental matters, when it come to world economic issues Canada is part of the U.S.: USCAN, in the words of Michael Vlahos.[16]

Vlahos is quoted here not only because, as far as we know, he coined the term USCAN but also because of the casual manner in which he asserts — "assumes" may be a better word — the identity of interests between Canada and the United States. This assumption has been part of American (but by no means only American) policy projections at least since the North American economic boom that followed the First World War. It has been the premise for praise, platitudes, sometimes consternation and even irritation, but rarely serious analysis. This is interesting in that all of Canadian history, including the very invention of Canada itself, speaks to the opposite. It is precisely because there was no identity of interest that Canada was founded in the first place. It is thus not without irony that to the extent that the world moves to establish and consolidate permanent trading blocs Canada will perforce become USCAN. Only in this context do some of the long and detailed stipulations of both the Canada-U.S. Free Trade Agreement and the North American Free Trade Agreement about what is and what isn't a product of North America make some sense.

Both the Canada-U.S. FTA and NAFTA are long, detailed, indeed convoluted treaties more than a thousand pages long, containing thousands of clauses and subsections, the burden of most of which are exclusions. Key parts of these two agreements, which exist ostensibly to promote free trade, are in fact highly protectionist: they seek to exclude components from other continents with the aim of achieving some standard of North American purity in the final product. In the auto industry (see chapter six), NAFTA actually raises to 62.5 per cent the proportion by value of components that have to come from North American sources for the finished vehicles to be considered North American and thus eligible for tariff-free movement between the signatory countries. This isn't free trade: this is protectionism aimed to suit local auto parts suppliers and the Detroit automakers with their substantial in-house production of components.

In the garment industry, the fabric that goes into finished clothing not only has to come from North American mills to meet NAFTA rules of origin, but the thread that goes into this fabric has to be North American as well — a triumph for the textile lobby but not for free trade. Canadian clothing manufacturers have won a partial exemption: although they face many competitive disadvantages vis-à-vis U.S. garment makers, one strength of several of the more successful firms has been an ability to seek out and incorporate European or Asian fabrics of sophisticated designs not duplicated in North America, particularly for men's suits. Under NAFTA, Canadian clothing exporters will continue to enjoy a small U.S. quota for imports containing exotic fabrics, but with little room for growth. The letter P for protectionism should perhaps be added somewhere to the initials of the FTA and NAFTA.

The main feature of both agreements is that they are duly signed and sealed and they have not really been negotiated yet. All the hard stuff about what is a subsidy as well as the trading regimes has yet to be agreed on and enacted. Canada's hands are tied in the sense that government economic, trade and social policies must still meet the unknown or unagreed test of what the Americans would consider "unfair trade practices." Rules governing these were to be negotiated and settled within five to seven years. In the meantime, the U.S. is able to use any countervail measures it sees fit, and there is only a dispute settlement panel to determine if the U.S. is applying its own laws correctly. Under NAFTA, the code that is supposed to determine what subsidies are to be allowed is postponed indefinitely.

This is perhaps one of the reasons why it has been impossible to determine the actual effect the FTA has had on the Canadian economy. It hasn't been negotiated yet. Meanwhile, a serious recession has intervened and the integration of the Canadian economy into the American continues to make the issue moot. It is moot in the automobile industry — it is as difficult to speak now of a Canadian automobile industry as it is to speak of an Ohio automobile industry. There are factories making automobiles in Ontario just as there are in Ohio — they make the same cars for the same companies. It is moot in the air transport industry, which is about to be integrated into the American system. It is moot in rail transport, which is concentrating on realigning routes into the U.S. grid. It is also moot in a perverse way in the steel industry: still independent, still competing with the U.S., and still being hit with countervail.

President Clinton described Canada as a "tiny country ... but one which trades more with [the U.S.] than Japan." Clinton went on to use the Canadian example as a benefit of free trade in that it increases trade within the bloc, apparently in and of itself a good thing. What is left unsaid is that trade within a given bloc must develop primarily to the exclusion of interbloc trading.

In early February 1993 the Canadian government released trade figures that quickly became the "good news of the day." Exports were up to the United States; indeed they were up generally, although the figures indicated trade redirection more than growth — the U.S. now accounts for 77 per cent of Canada's exports (up from 73 per cent just before the FTA).[17] Less frequently mentioned in the one-day euphoria was the fact that the released statistics counted only trade in goods. If services, interest payments, dividend flows and other transactions are counted, Canada continues to run a trade deficit of enormous and increasing proportions. According to Giles Gherson, then of the *Financial Times of Canada*, even with the surplus in goods, Canada's current account deficit was in the neighbourhood of $30 billion.[18] In addition, these figures could also indicate a decline in economic activity in that raw materials manufactured in Canada would not necessarily be reflected in trade figures. There is plenty of scope for statistical legerdemain in instances where raw materials formerly incorporated in Canadian-made goods are instead shipped south for processing and show up as part of an increase in exports.

Figures can now be twisted into the invention of a "jobless recovery" (a contradiction in terms that makes other pronouncements such as "less is more" lucid and logical), but the actual state of Canada's economy in the post-free trade era is hardly open to dispute. It is also undisputed that the country, provinces, regions, crown corporations and private individuals face a mountain of debt and an enormous tax burden that not only undermines the country's longer-term economic prospects but also threatens a full-blown currency crisis at any moment.

The dominant figure in Canadian economic policy over the last nine years, Michael Wilson, used to like to call the Canada-U.S. Free

Trade Agreement not a trade bloc but rather a building block of increased international trade. In other words globalism — the fabled nirvana — was to be reached incrementally, cells spreading out, something like an ink stain on a blotter. It should be pointed out that Wilson was almost alone in this sophistry. Not quite, however. The ever-faithful *Globe and Mail* sees NAFTA as a magnet with "countries across Latin America — and beyond — scrambling over each other to join NAFTA. . . . Thus free trade's domino effect: bilateralism becomes minilateralism becomes multilateralism."[19]

Despite such obfuscation, Michael Wilson set Canada's economic and, perhaps, political direction in a straightforward and decisive way. In a 1992 speech he put the issue directly:

> The world's thirty-first largest population did not become and cannot sustain the world's eighth largest economy without expanding its base beyond its domestic market, now twenty-seven million people.
>
> By opening our economy to greater competition from U.S.-based firms, by encouraging Canadian-based firms to serve both the U.S. and Canadian markets and exposing them to the discipline of meeting greater competition both here in Canada and in new U.S. markets, the FTA provided Canadian firms, particularly manufacturing firms, with the impetus to adopt global business strategies.
>
> The companies that are closing, the jobs we are losing, are in most cases, companies and jobs that could not adjust to meet the tough reality of a global economy. I take no satisfaction in making this point, but it is a point we must never forget.
>
> That is why Canadians must be in the forefront in every major trade negotiation. We live by trade and are critically dependent on the rules. We insist on a seat at every trade negotiating table because our future depends upon it.[20]

One supposes that Wilson's approach could be considered by some as a form of economic "tough love," but it has been a failure nevertheless. And as one examines the extent of the failure, the nature of the trap Canada has set for itself, and the inevitable consequences, become clearer.

Canada's Free Trade Schizophrenia

Free trade — or, as it was called at the time, freer trade — was originally seen even by the Canadian government in more modest terms, as basically a defensive device to protect Canada's economy from the ravages of American protectionism. The idea that Canada and the U.S. were to be partners in the creation of the new global economy came only as the decibel level of the free trade debate increased. This notion, which is strangely enough still alive in the wreckage of the Canadian economy, can be illustrated by some of the eulogies given the retiring Prime Minister Mulroney:

> Negotiating free trade with the United States took courage. It imposed restructuring upon Canadian industry to make it competitive in today's global economy. The short-term pain, measured by unemployment and bankruptcies — was severe. Rising exports to the United States, though, hold out the promise of long-term gain.[21]

Under various names, free trade with the United States has always been a goal of Canadian economic policy. It has also always been a dicier question politically. As soon as free trade is mentioned, the obvious questions of customs union, monetary union and political union arise. This is, of course, natural: free trade means a common market and a common market is the *sine qua non* of the modern nation-state. This is what all the shouting is about in Europe at the moment.

For Canada — whose independent existence the United States has, both serially and concurrently, considered a threat, a nuisance, sometimes to be useful, more often to be ignored — free trade with the U.S. is both logical and life-threatening. That is why historically Canada has always been both the "demandeur" and the "rejecter."

Thus, in Wilfrid Laurier's day, the dangers of reciprocity vis-à-vis the United States could be somehow mitigated by the still powerful British Empire and more precisely by Britain's Canadian holdings and equity investments, as well as by the fact that Canada still did, and would as long as the Empire survived, have what it lacked in the 1980s — what Pierre Trudeau in a different context called a third option. Yet the fear of the long-term implications of reciprocity, particularly among the railway interests who rightly feared the north-south continental pull, overcame all other enthusiasms for the market opportunities President William Howard Taft presented. While the nascent industrial class of Ontario gets much of the blame for the 1911 rejection of reciprocity, it was the CPR's William Van Horne in Montreal whose order was most succinct: "Bust this thing."[22]

While this third option existed, it could be argued that a reciprocity agreement with the U.S. could actually strengthen Canadian independence in that it would provide an economic counterbalance to British influence. Thus, as Mackenzie King brooded alone about the free trade agreement negotiated but unsigned between Canada and the United States in 1948, he realized he had no British counterlever. To his diary he confided that he was warned off the deal by the ghost of Sir Wilfrid, which brought him to the realization that the American aim had always been Manifest Destiny. Apparently he was helped in this realization by a U.S. leak to *Life* magazine, whose publisher Henry Luce (whom King detested) was already touting the deal as a precursor to annexation. In rejecting the FTA of 1948, King tried to breathe some life into the British Commonwealth. But the world had moved past the Empire.

The draft outline of the 1948 agreement was a few thousand words, about four typeset pages. It began with simple, rather straightforward statements such as "immediate removal of all customs duties." It was negotiated quietly, without fanfare, indeed in secret — probably so that the parties concerned could see if such a deal was possible. Without going into the whys and wherefores of the 1948 negotiations, it is interesting to observe the methodology employed and contrast it with that of the current agreements.

Part of the reason for the increased complexity of these agreements may have been indicated by Lloyd Bentsen, then a Texas senator (now with presumably more clout as Secretary of the Treasury), who protested Canada's very involvement in the free trade negotiations with Mexico. In his argument he compared the American goal of hemispheric free trade to a wheel. The U.S. is the hub and Canada merely one of the spokes in what is intended to be a many-spoked wheel. While in some ways apt, the hub-spoke analogy is not a very happy one for Canada. The Canadian economy is much too similar to the American and much too integrated into it to be considered distinct even to the limited extent that a spoke is distinct from the hub. Free trade between Canada and the U.S. could be considered by optimists as some sort of partnership, but it is a partnership described by some, notably former prime minister Pierre Trudeau, as that between a mouse and an elephant. Not a marriage, says former ambassador to the United States Charles Ritchie, but "an arrangement."

The need, therefore, was to negotiate a free trade agreement that wasn't a free trade agreement. As "demandeur" Canada spent most of its negotiating capital on "keeping things off the table," while the Americans countered with "the level playing field" — both nondescriptions of nonissues. What finally emerged was a massive document that more than anything else skirted the issue of free trade itself. Thus after four years of a phasing-in period, nobody can say with any assurance what the overall economic effect has been.

But the essential burden of both the FTA and NAFTA is that Canada is part of the American domestic market, as Mexico now is as well. In the case of Mexico and the rest of Latin America, however, the traditional attitude of the U.S. is best reflected in the famous Monroe Doctrine. While making Latin America a protectorate, the U.S. did recognize its independence or quasi-independence. The attitude towards Canada is, however, simply incomprehension over a historical quirk and a series of political and military blunders and accidents that created the temporary anomaly of two countries sharing the land mass that should be one. American trade actions under the FTA have generally made two points:

• Canada is part of the domestic market and any areas where there is even a modicum of competition that could not be consistent within the context of one domestic market, such as Canadian action to preserve its "cultural industries," airlines, transportation, even steel, should be discouraged and fought. The most important phrase in the whole agreement is "national treatment." Canadians tend to concentrate the meaning of this in areas of energy. The Americans have a much broader interpretation. To illustrate this point, consider the American reaction if the subsidies Canadian governments freely give the big three automobile corporations (by one count, it comes to $64 million or about $7,300 per worker) were to be given to a non-American corporation (Honda) or to Canadian-owned competitor to an American corporation (steel).

• Canada, and now Mexico, are to be prevented from being a platform for Japan and Europe to penetrate the American domestic market. The message to the Japanese is that if you want to build a Honda factory to service the American market, you had better locate it in the U.S. — unless you have the prior approval of one of the Big Three in the form of a joint venture.

The U.S. is still armed with enough legislative weapons to stop the importation of anything dead in its tracks. And when Congress runs out of "trade remedies," it simply creates more. It has now revived something called Super 301 legislation, which allows Washington to retaliate against countries that in its judgement trade unfairly. Unfair trade in the eyes of Americans, as we have seen in steel, lumber, pork and wheat (just about everything Canada trades with the U.S. that is not a subsidiary operation), is a wide-ranging and many splendoured thing. Now they will have in Super 301 an all-purpose retroactive declaration of a trade war to be used whenever and against whomever they want.

Trade barriers against foreign competition are as American as apple pie and urban riots. Canada has traditionally not opposed American restrictions. It has, rather, sought exemptions or formal free trade agreements. Canada's trade policy towards the U.S. has never been ambiguous, merely schizophrenic. It has striven always to be conjoined with the American economic system — to be part of it but not of it. To paraphrase a former prime minister, not necessarily economic integration but economic integration if necessary. Not in any way shape or form (some half-hearted pro-forma protestations excepted) did Canada protest American protectionism in theory, principle or practice. Canada's motive, therefore, in being, as far as the public were appraised, the demandeur in negotiations on free (freer) trade was not to join some global movement to advance world trading freedom — Canada was a card-carrying member of GATT — but to get inside the walls of Fortress America that it saw abuilding. The political rhetoric (unfortunately, on both sides of the issue) obscured both the reality of the North American economy and Canada's options within this reality.

Canada achieved what it set out to achieve — with the possible exception of one totally unreasonable assumption: that the FTA would represent some truly mutual, equal and monogamous affair. Even the so-called surrender of control over natural resources and energy was part of the opening gambit, not some last-ditch concession. The problem is not that Canada didn't fully achieve what it wanted (or was told it wanted) out of the negotiations — the bemused and confused grin on U.S. negotiator Peter Murphy's face no doubt grew out of his inability to understand Simon Reisman's hysterical refusal to take yes for an answer — but that Canada's goals were the wrong goals.

Nationalism and continentalism have coexisted in all Canadian political parties (with the exception of the NDP, which expelled its organized nationalist wing), but there has never been any doubt that when the issue became critical Canadians became continentalists. While America was dominant, everyone could afford an independent Canada. Indeed, it was often politically useful to the United States in UN peacekeeping functions, NATO compromises and G-7 negotiations for an independent Canada to be free to act as a surrogate. While it is perhaps not of the same order, there is a similarity between Canada's position in organizations such as the G-7 and the seats of the old Soviet Ukraine and Byelorussia in the United Nations. In this regard Spain's interest in taking Canada's seat at the G-7 may not be entirely frivolous. When the G-7 was the G-5, Italy, by counting its "unofficial" economy together with its official one, claimed Britain's chair. That, in fact, is how the group grew: Britain was allowed to save face and Italy and Canada got to be members. Canadian membership may not now be as important as it once was.

How Canada examined and exercised its options concerning its independent coexistence on the continent with the United States is an interesting historical question. Perhaps there never really were any long-term options (as distinct from desires). This certainly would seem to be the logic of those who support the present course. And there is plenty of historical, cultural and economic evidence to support them. Even before there was either a Canada or a United States, the predominant idea was that North America was to be one economic and political entity. This was especially true after the elimination of French rule on the continent. Even when Britain was the dominant economic and military power, its Canadian outpost was always vulnerable, at least in the minds of everyone who cared to notice. Perhaps vulnerable is the wrong word: maybe inevitable suits better the historical circumstances.

Therefore, with the coming of the "new globalism" and the triumph of the liberal theories of political economy, Canada seems perfectly positioned to be one of the first sovereignties to become unsovereign — in particular since its intended is not just any old country but the United States, the pole of the unipolar world. This would be especially true if America's relationship to the industrialized world were going through a change and there were a new reality of trading blocs with economic and political integration within them. Then Canada also faces a new reality in which being part way in the American tent — according to latest trade figures, it is more than 70 per cent in — will not be adequate. To protect, even enhance, Canada's regional economies, it would need to be fully integrated, including eventual political integration into a new United States of America.

Strategy for Survival

It is one thing to project the inevitability of the political disintegration of Canada. But a central problem with NAFTA is the fear that it could weaken and undermine living standards, and by forcing this downward competition make any fight back more difficult.

The industrial economy of North America has been taking a very serious battering, and by current projections coming at us from all sides will continue to take a battering. The Canadian Labour Congress estimates that Canada has lost 350,000 jobs since the FTA was signed. The actual numbers are not in dispute; the argument is about the cause. One is tempted to suggest that we have been lied to, but to suggest that would imply that somebody knew the truth. We can await the autopsy to apportion blame as to the recession, economic restructuring or whatever, but even *The Economist*, whose enthusiasm for agreements such as the FTA and NAFTA knows bounds only when they stray away from market principles into areas of a social compact, admitted the "devastation" was "certainly aggravated.... . Many Canadians expect NAFTA to carry the demolition of Canada's manufacturing industry further, especially in Ontario."[23]

Moreover, since the North American economy slipped into the recession years before the rest of the world, its trade position has been weakened in relation to Europe and Japan. This gave a veneer of economic justification to the FTA and NAFTA — a Fortress America to protect the continent from the predatory economies of Europe and Asia. This was just a light veneer because a free trade agreement that is actually an agreement to close one's borders to competition is a contradiction.

But NAFTA is not just an economic agreement but also a political tool to enforce classical liberal economics and politics on a world that has outgrown them by two centuries. In a remarkable article in the Toronto *Star*, "Kissinger's 'truly New World Order,'" reporter Linda Diebel developed the actual genesis of both NAFTA and the U.S.-Canada Free Trade Agreement (NAFTA was the goal, the original Canada-U.S. talks merely a sideshow). From the beginning (the notion that Canada initiated the talks) to the end (Mexico didn't enter the picture until the original agreement was settled), the whole process as presented to the Canadian people was a tissue of lies.

Describing the whole process as "a straightforward corporate strategy ... part of a larger plan for U.S. hemispheric hegemony, which [Henry] Kissinger calls 'a revolutionary concept ... a truly new world order'":

> Its basic premise is no-holds-barred free enterprise for all the Americas. Big business would set the rules; there would be few or no regulations to impede industry. It would be the survival of the fittest.

> Of course, society would have to change. According to [David] Rockefeller, "We face serious and persistent patterns of thought and behavior that require modification if a free trade system is to function effectively."[24]

Diebel rounds up the usual suspects when capitalism at its most nefarious is being discussed. David Rockefeller and Henry Kissinger lead the pack. There are some corporate executives including James Robinson III, formerly of *Barbarians at the Gate* and American Express and of an apparently surviving friendship with Brian Mulroney. There is also the chairman of Caterpillar Inc., Donald Fites, who during a recent and very important strike victory over the United Automobile Workers emphasized that the wage issue in the U.S. is to get level with the Mexicans, although differences in productivity levels and other factors make this unlikely. There is also the usual supporting cast of gofers with big titles such as Thomas D'Aquino of the Business Council on National Issues and Right Honourable flunkies such as Brian Mulroney and others talking about concepts of "pooling sovereignty."

But things may not work out that way. As both Robbie Burns and Mick Jagger have noted, "You can't always get what you want." A whole series of problems are coming to the fore with NAFTA. And like GATT, NAFTA may not be worth the trouble and even concessions the United States may be forced to make to keep the process going. It is clear, for example, that Mexico is demanding a different arrangement for its petroleum resources from the one the U.S. is prepared to concede Canada. Internal American political pressure for environmental and worker protection can also threaten to impinge on the already negotiated FTA.

And other circumstances have changed. There is both a continuum and a departure in American trade policy. The U.S. is now ready to confront both Europe and Japan and seems ready to undertake a full-scale trade war if necessary. Turning its back finally on neoconservative economics, which has left painful after-effects in Britain, Canada and the U.S., the Clinton administration is buttressing a new aggressive trade policy — "strategic trade" — with a new industrial policy whose essence includes the marginalization of so-called joint initiatives such as the FTA and NAFTA, and even GATT, in favour of American unilateralism. At this early stage, it appears to be a movement beyond the defensive posture of Fortress America towards a challenge to both Europe and Japan. "Strategic trade" is the Americans doing what the Japanese have been doing in all branches of high technology and what the Europeans have also been doing specifically with Airbus — creating an industrial strategy around key sectors of the economy and then using the power of the state to finance development and blast them into international markets. We are talking here not about multilateral talks and ludicrous "win-win" scenarios, but about unilateral moves and countermoves. It is a strategy that takes no prisoners. It does, however, have a number of hostages — notably Canada.

When President Clinton talks about the need to rebuild America's economy, he is not talking about Canada's. When he talks about saving Boeing from Airbus, he does not include Canadair. When the steel industry needs protection, it is the steel industry of the United States: Canada is part of the enemy. The Americans are interesting in that way. There are times when we are one happy continent, and there are other times when the forty-ninth parallel could be the Berlin Wall.

We get some indication of how this works from the juxtaposition of two events that occurred within days of each other in 1992: the massive restructuring and downsizing of General Motors and the curious decision of the U.S. Customs Service to challenge the right of Canadian-assembled Hondas to enter the U.S. tariff-free (see chapter six). Interestingly enough, both events called forth the by now standard Japan-bashing. Bob White, then president of the Canadian Auto Workers, called for government action to force Honda to import less and build more vehicles in Canada. In the wake of the GM decision, several NDP MPs called upon the government to restrict Japanese auto sales in Canada.

If the message to the Japanese is that investment in Canada is not the way into the North American market, the Japanese are likely to oblige. In the case of GM, Canada's independence is acknowledged in the sense that the cuts in Canada were proportionately larger than those made in the U.S. On the other hand, since the continent is integrated, the fact that GM in Canada is very profitable and that the plant slated for closure is efficient and competitive means nothing. In the new global economic restructuring, efficiency and competitiveness mean a great deal, but being part of head office means everything.

The United States is very much like a 900-pound gorilla: it does basically what it wants to do. Canadians can laissez-faire themselves to death and recite *The Wealth of Nations* in the *Report on Business* every morning, but if the U.S. engages in an industrial strategy, the Canadian economy will be sideswiped if Canada does not react. The best way to react would be to establish an industrial strategy of its own and get on with an active policy of entering into free trade agreements with anybody and everybody who will join.

The issue is not free trade versus protectionism. Protectionism is not an option for Canada. It has, in fact, no market to protect. Canada's livelihood is based on trade and it has two ways to get into the modern world trading system, on its own or as part of the United States. We think the current agreements Canada is rushing to sign move it away from independent free trade while at the same time it is in danger of losing the protection provided for it within the American tent. *The Economist* suggested a test as to whether NAFTA furthered the concept of free trade or weakened it.[25] The test was simple. Turn the agreement into the beginnings of world free trade by inviting off-continent nations — *The Economist* mentioned Poland and Taiwan — to join. Why not indeed?

In this context we can try to answer the question posed about Canada's defection from the American bloc. While Canada cannot jump out of its own continent or skin, it is also a Pacific nation. The key to Canada's prosperity is to expand its trading and commercial relations with Japan and the other countries of the Pacific Rim: to remain part of America, to become part of a properly organized and negotiated NAFTA, but at the same time to break out of the restrictive covenants of the agreement as it now stands — in other words to be integrated fully within North America but to reject the Fortress America concept by maintaining Canada's freedom to become part of a global trading system.

If the creation of trading blocs is antithetical to free trade, if they are superstates in formation, the new globalism is merely the old globalism with fewer players. Canada then has no future, except to become a more or less identifiable region of North America. However, if the trading blocs can be undermined and the world truly moves in the direction of a free trading regime, then Canada has as much chance and as much reason to survive as a distinct entity as any country on earth. And those are not bad odds.

Chapter 6

Four Key Industries

The effects of the emergence of trade blocs, and the narrowing possibilities open to Canada, can be seen from another angle by looking at specific sectors of the economy. In this chapter we examine four: automobile manufacturing, steel making, air transport and agriculture. All have been characterized by special arrangements that now have broken down or are under threat. In all of them, the Canada-U.S. Free Trade Agreement and other moves towards continental integration have proved a mixed blessing, and recent reality has not matched the hopes held out a few short years ago.

Auto: A North American Industry

American subsidiaries play a major role in many Canadian industries, but there are few cases in which the degree of dominance has been total as in motor vehicles.

— Carl E. Beigie,
The Canada-U.S. Automotive Agreement: An Evaluation[1]

In a sense, the notion of something called the Canadian automobile industry is misleading. Hundreds of thousands of automobiles are produced yearly in Canada, but they are produced in plants completely owned by American parents and totally integrated into the single North American automobile market.[2] And this has almost always been the case.

In the last decade of the nineteenth century, just about every carriage maker and tinkerer — in Canada, in the United States and, for that matter, throughout industrialized Europe — was experimenting with the horseless carriage. According to one historian, Toronto produced Canada's first electric vehicle in 1893, and the first gasoline buggy was manufactured in Hamilton in 1898.[3] The development of the self-propelled vehicle was a simultaneous occurrence throughout the then-industrialized world, and Canada was a part of this phenomenon, as both a manufacturer and a market.

But almost from the moment of their inception, the Canadian industry and market merged with their larger American counterparts. The sixth automobile produced by Ford in Detroit was purchased by a Windsor doctor in 1903. Within a year of this purchase, Ford had incorporated itself in Canada and was manufacturing hundreds of automobiles before Colonel Sam McLaughlin started mass production by installing the Buick engine in his Oshawa-built carriages. When General Motors was organized and Buick became part of this trust, McLaughlin became General Motors of Canada. By 1911 there were nineteen automobile companies manufacturing in Ontario, but only eight, all of them American (Durant, Star, Flint, Gray Dort, Reo and Studebaker, as well as GM and Ford), survived the decade. These firms became part of the rationalization of the North American industry and were eventually incorporated into the Big Three. Studebaker survived as an independent until the late 1960s and for the last months of its existence had its total production shifted to its plant in Hamilton.

Thus, from its virtual beginnings, the automobile industry was continental. On the whole, automobile plants operating in Canada were no different from plants operating in various states of the American union. There was one distinction, which was important at the time: the Canadian tariff and the British imperial preference encouraged the fiction of an independent Canadian corporate structure and promoted manufacturing in Canada. The Canadian automobile industry became a platform for the export of American automobiles throughout the British Empire while at the same time servicing a section of the Canadian domestic market.

In some respects, the development of the auto industry was typical of the development of the branch-plant industrial economy of Canada, and especially in Ontario. But there were differences, one of them being the early and total American ownership we have already noted. The aircraft industry, for example, developed in roughly the same period. The first interurban flight was between Toronto and Hamilton, yet aircraft manufacturing developed mainly through subsidiaries of British firms. In agriculture, Canada's pioneering corporations — Massey, Harris, Cockshutt and others — developed, competed and maintained their independence until a sectoral free trade agreement and worldwide slump in agriculture finally did them in. But what primarily distinguished automobile manufacturing in the twentieth century was its rapid growth and its almost total domination of the industrial economy. Auto assembly and manufacture represent only part of the industry's reach. Just about every product manufactured — steel, rubber, electrical, ceramics, plastic — is a component or ancillary part of an automobile, not to mention the highways, roads, bridges and tunnels.

As the Canadian industry developed, it specialized in a limited number of models, while other models reflecting the full range of production the market demanded had to be imported from the U.S. under an increasingly complicated system of tariffs and rebates. Canadian plants were less and less capable of serving the Canadian market, and the overall Canadian trade deficit, fuelled by the demand for imported American-produced models and parts, grew to crisis proportions. Meanwhile, the imperial preference grew meaningless, eventually to disappear altogether in the Common Market.

Various studies — of particular note the Bladen Commission in 1961 — sensed that the long-term survival of automobile production in Canada depended on even closer integration with the American parent. The balance-of-payments crisis dictated the removal of the border in automobile manufacturing and trade. The 1965 Auto Pact provided for Canada-U.S. free trade in automobiles and auto parts, allowing the U.S.-based giants to rationalize production on a continental basis. Free trade was, however, made dependent on a number of "safeguards" for the segment of the industry located in Canada, which ensured that production would remain above a base level and would increase along with increasing sales in Canada.

This is not to suggest that there was no opposition to the Auto Pact at the time of its negotiation. There were proposals for an "all-Canadian" car, a restructuring of the industry, even its nationalization, but even without the benefit of hindsight these alternatives were illusory.

It would be very difficult to imagine a single Canadian car dominating a market so closely connected with the United States. The simple fact is that since the birth of the industry there has been a single North American market, and there was no way that market was to be split by the creation of a Canadian car in the mid-1960s. Moreover, full integration of the Canadian industry with the American could prove beneficial to the American owners by increasing the efficiency of Canadian production and allowing them to take full advantage of the subsidy represented by Canadian social programs as well as lower Canadian wages. The Auto Pact was seen as a favour to Canadians as well as a bonus to the American owners, and so it was. If Canada gave up any quest for an independent industry, it also received assurances of continued jobs and a promised share of production.

Moreover, with full integration, the Canadian operations could not really be considered branch plants. They were as much a part of the whole skein of North American operations as a plant anywhere in the continental U.S. Indeed, with structural changes in the industry, the smaller and more efficient Canadian plants could compete with American ones. Free trade, as we are finding out every day, eliminates the economic need and rationale for a branch-plant operation. However, a fully integrated economy does not necessarily imply that plants would not operate in Canada — or even grow, especially in expansionary times.

And in generally expansionary times, this has been the experience with the U.S.-Canada Auto Pact. After almost thirty years of the pact's existence, the manufacture and assembly of automobiles and parts remains at a high level in Canada. Indeed, even now, NAFTA and various grumblings of House Majority Leader Richard Gephardt and others notwithstanding, the Big Three's Canadian plants operate under much the same circumstances as their other domestic production facilities. That is, with one crucial political distinction: the Canadian automobile industry may be part of the domestic American industry, Canadian automobile workers may be part of the domestic industrial workforce, but Canada elects no one to the U.S. Senate or House of Representatives and has, as yet, no votes in the U.S. electoral college.

This distinction hasn't been too important over the years as it has been generally understood that what has been good for General Motors has been good for America — all of America, including Canada. And until now (and indeed as long as labour costs remain lower in Canada and the tricky questions of "what are subsidies" remain unnegotiated in the free trade deals), the Auto Pact has been very good to GM, Chrysler and Ford. (It is widely believed that the Canadian operations saved Chrysler in the 1970s and they are certainly the main underpinning of its successful minivans and LH models.) How highly the American corporate headquarters value the Auto Pact was expressed in 1971, when they overruled President Richard Nixon's decision to annul the agreement.

The automobile has been described as an "intermediate technology" and has been written off by many. In the United States, more people are involved in the computer industry than are directly involved in automobile production. American economist Lester Thurow considers it an open question whether any American automobile firm can last another twenty years.[4] The trouble with Thurow and his predictions is that he is not always wrong. But while automobile production today may be considered a "mature" industry, by some even a declining one, the auto is still at the very core of Canadian industrial production. Indeed, the steel industry, where the proportion of Canadian ownership is almost exactly the same as the proportion of American ownership in the auto industry, has seen its exports to the United States decline considerably since the FTA.

There is no doubt that the auto industry is rapidly changing. It is becoming much more capital-intensive and less labour-intensive. Where once Henry Ford would announce that his customers could choose any colour of car they wanted as long as it was black, there are now any number of models and variants. Individual market niches have long since replaced the basic Ford and Chevy. In this sense, the market may prove Thurow right. Economies of scale and long production runs created giants such as General Motors. Market changes may now dictate that they break into clusters of almost boutique manufacturers. In some respects, the proliferation of models and variants has helped the Canadian segment of the industry, in that Canada's relatively small plants can more easily adapt to the fragmentation of the market.

However, there are some disturbing signals on the horizon. Canada is still a foreign country, and as the American industry downsizes, faces competition in its domestic market from the Japanese and the Europeans, and generally goes through market contractions, there is little or no political fallout from closing a foreign facility. The hit GM gave Canada in its most recent batch of closures was proportionately rather large. More interestingly, the existence or nonexistence of the Auto Pact was not even mentioned.

When GM closed its van assembly plant in Toronto in early 1993, it did not dispute that, of all the facilities producing the vehicle, the Toronto plant was the most efficient and profitable. In one of the more baffling non sequiturs to come out of business circles, one corporate executive claimed that "efficiency does not play an important part in GM's worldwide downsizing program." The same official went on to explain that "the company is trying to reduce the cost of manufacturing vehicles in North America."[5]

If in an effort to "cut costs," a company closes an efficient operation to consolidate in a less efficient one, the costs we are talking about may be political rather than financial. The plant being expanded is in Flint, Michigan, which as more than one observer noticed was the setting of the documentary satire on GM, *Roger and Me*. GM made its decision the same week as Mack Truck reached a deal with its American workers on a new concessionary contract by agreeing to discontinue production in Oakville. Had that agreement concerned the closure of an American plant, there would have been plenty of political fallout. As it was, there was none. Nor was it only Canadians who were affected. A few weeks later, GM announced that it was moving a thousand jobs from Mexico to a plant in Lansing, Michigan.

Although it happens with ever less frequency, from time to time Canadians are told that they are really not Americans. The message that Canada was not the United States was conveyed to the Japanese owners of Honda, and every other Japanese and European who was listening. When Honda attempted to use the Free Trade Agreement as a means to enable Canadian production to enter the American market, the Americans cried foul and reinterpreted content regulations to make its Canadian-assembled products ineligible for duty-free export to the U.S. It is not that Honda does not have production facilities in the United States. It has very large ones — Hondas are now exported from the U.S. to Japan. The Americans are simply making two points. First, even the largest corporations are subject to political pressures in recessionary times. And second, of at least equal importance, if a product is not manufactured in the United States or by an American corporation, it cannot be guaranteed hassle-free entry into the American market, free trade or no free trade. Canada knows this from its experience in steel, softwood lumber, pork bellies, and just about everything else, where non-tariff barriers are higher now than before the FTA.

For the Japanese and the Europeans, the message is: if existing content rules don't apply, new ones can be made up as we go along. Content rules can, for example, be made to apply to the company's advertising budget, the mortgage on its plant, just about anything a lobbyist in Washington can invent. While Honda and Volkswagen were audited and hounded in Canada, down the road in Ingersoll, Ontario, Suzuki and GM were merrily assembling little sports vehicles for the North American market. And in St. Thomas, Ford was using another loophole in content regulations to export Crown Victorias into the United States.

At the core, economics are politics. This may not be as obvious in good times as in times of decline or challenge and change. The Auto Pact was a solution to a mainly Canadian problem in the boom period of the Vietnam war when President Johnson vowed to produce guns and butter, but it was not entirely a generous gesture. It was certainly in the interests of the automobile companies, it helped meet the production demands brought about by the war, and politically, as Johnson adviser George Ball put it, it set a pattern for the full integration of the Canadian industrial economy into the American.

But as Lord Melbourne once observed, "no country has eternal friends or enemies, only eternal interests." And the interests of the U.S. are now ill served by trade arrangements with its neighbours that guarantee national production levels. That is why under NAFTA, the content regulations are generalized to North America, not divided among the countries that make up the agreement.

When NAFTA was first being negotiated, representatives of the three countries found themselves seriously at odds in trying to determine how high they should set the minimum level of North American components that automobiles would have to contain to be considered North American products under the terms of the deal. There was a fundamental difference of view between the Detroit Big Three and everyone else, and the U.S. negotiators essentially adopted the Detroit position. Ever eager to stifle competition not only from Japanese imports but also from Japanese-owned plants in North America, Detroit wanted this minimum content level raised to the sky, since the vehicles they make on their home turf contain more North American parts than anything coming from the Japanese-owned plants.

Under the Auto Pact the minimum level had been pegged at 50 per cent. It was this provision the Americans used to disrupt U.S. sales of Canadian-made Hondas, alleging that the North American content of these vehicles fell slightly below 50 per cent. Under NAFTA this minimum actually rises to 62.5 per cent — not as high as Detroit was shooting for, but higher than either Canada or Mexico favoured.

As the NAFTA negotiators argued over percentages, it hardly seemed to occur to them that, if they really were serious about free trade, they should be seeking to eliminate these content rules altogether. The provision they negotiated instead raised, not lowered, the obstacles to overseas trade. If North American component makers can compete in price and quality in every instance, then they have no need for protection in the form of minimum content rules. If overseas producers can sometimes provide cheaper and better components, then the North American vehicles that contain these components will also be cheaper and better and should be more competitive both at home and abroad. And if North American auto parts makers are sheltered from overseas competition, then they are inviting retaliation that will shut them out of promising new markets in the future while encouraging more Japanese and European component makers to set up shop in North America in direct competition with them, thus making for a more thinly sliced pie. This is not a brilliant step, but then again foresight has not been a Detroit hallmark, and the NAFTA partners are the poorer for it.

Another lever Canada had under the Auto Pact to influence the development of the industry will be removed under NAFTA. If Canadians want to, they can affect the direction of the industry through subsidies and loans, which are now routine in the industry. In 1993 Ontario gave several million dollars to the now profitable Chrysler Corporation without the guarantee of one new job, while GM in Sainte-Thérèse, Quebec, is a full-time corporate welfare bum. The last time Chrysler was on the verge of bankruptcy, both the Ontario and federal governments were asked to participate in the bailout. In the negotiations, led in Ontario by Tory cabinet minister Larry Grossman and federally by Liberal cabinet minister Herb Gray, a deal with Chrysler was forged that forced the company to direct its investments towards modernizing its Canadian operations and to earmark funds towards research and development in Canada.[6]

If we are talking about industrial integration, which is implicit in free trade, then research and engineering facilities can be established anywhere. Toyota has just built a massive research facility in Michigan that could have just as easily been built in Ontario. The problem is the lack of political will, or rather in Canada the ideological stupor of the political authorities who equate free trade with laissez-faire and thus seek to force opponents of their Thatcherite economic nonsense into a defensive protectionist posture.

Globalism and free trade combine very effectively with government intervention and direction. A case in point is Japan, Germany, every successful modern economy. Even the U.S. is getting the point. A negative example is Britain, whose domestic automobile industry has been destroyed. It is now seeing a slight revival with new Japanese assembly plants, but rather than a revitalization of a British industry the Japanese branch plants merely make Britain, in the eyes of the Europeans, a Japanese aircraft carrier — a platform for export into Europe.[7]

For Canada, the issue stands differently. With its relatively small and efficient plants, experienced and well-educated workforce and strategic location, Canada can take advantage of the fragmenting automobile market by developing an industrial policy that will encourage Japanese investment. Canada has considerable leverage here in that Japan has for the past decade been its second most important trading partner. The U.S. has already served notice that it intends to broaden NAFTA to include other countries in Latin America, and there is talk now of broadening it further to include countries of the Pacific Rim. Canada's experience with the Auto Pact and FTA shows that the U.S. has full sovereign control over its trade and industrial policy, and the argument once advanced that the FTA guaranteed full, secure and preferential access to the American market was never tenable. As NAFTA attempts to broaden out, the opportunity is there for Canada to enter into sectoral or full free trade agreements with Japan and other countries of the Pacific Rim. It is either that or continue to be a mere spoke in the American wheel.

Steel: The Problem of Geography

For Canada's major steel producers, it was a long, fast fall from enjoying the fruits of a low Canadian dollar and a superefficient technology to implosion and imminent bankruptcy. In 1980, given an eighty-five-cent dollar, Canadian steel companies enjoyed a $100-per-ton cost advantage over American producers. By 1990, this advantage had been wiped out.[8]

What intervened during this period? The Canada-United States Free Trade Agreement? The success of the new technology of the steel "minimills"? The consequent weakening of the American unions and a decrease in wages in the U.S. of between 10 and 20 per cent while Canadian workers gained wage increases 10 to 20 per cent greater than the rate of inflation? Probably a combination of factors, including the most important, the continental recession that tightened the market and put the squeeze on every producer.

Even if there are wage differentials, they could hardly reflect anything close to $100 a ton. Besides, labour costs generally have gone down, as employment in the steel industry in both Canada and the United States has been cut almost in half since 1980. Let us consider, then, the FTA and the new steel technology. At the time of writing, Dofasco had announced plans to close its old number one mill in Hamilton in the summer of 1993, at the cost of about 2,000 jobs. It will replace the production of number one mill with a new "minimill" built in the southern United States as a joint venture with another Canadian firm, Co-Steel of Toronto. It will be in a warm, rural setting with cheap electricity, access to highways and no unions — corporate paradise. And south of the border it will enjoy a hassle-free tariff environment. In other words, Dofasco will find the only real and secure method of entering the American steel market by becoming part of it.

The state of steel technology is roughly the same in Canada as in the United States (or, for that matter, any other industrial country). Canada has large integrated mills that are state-of-the-art and can compete in quality with the new minimills, which essentially recycle scrap metal. But these integrated mills require almost constant investment in an industry that even before the recession was, as they say, "mature." Canada also has modern minimills, as well as some old clunkers where taxpayers' dollars are shovelled into antiquated furnaces. But in Canada, the problem is not where the industry is technologically, but where it is geographically.

When the United States decided to protect its domestic steel industry from foreign competition, it invoked its "antidumping" laws. Canada was given no exemption although this was in clear violation of what we have been told is the spirit of the FTA. It did not violate the letter of the FTA because there is no letter. Details of the trading regime — what are subsidies, what is dumping, and the like — were to be negotiated over the first years of the agreement. In the meantime, all restrictive legislation would remain in effect and a mechanism would be established to determine whether this legislation was properly applied. This was a stopgap solution until the details could all be negotiated, or at least it was presented as such. However, the FTA was signed in 1988 and negotiations have not yet begun. Nor are they ever likely to because, as the United States made clear in 1988, it had no intention of signing any agreement that would remove authority from the U.S. government to enact any trade legislation it wants.

This American refusal to create a free market between Canada and the U.S. by guaranteeing access and the removal of non-tariff harassment was the crucial and central issue of the free trade negotiations, the issue that finally caused the talks to break down and forced the final concession from Brian Mulroney during the midnight heroics as the deadline neared. At the time, it was fobbed off on the Canadian people as a picky detail that would obstruct the "fast track procedure" and allow the "complex" deal to be nibbled away.[9] The Toronto *Globe and Mail* assured its readers that "American restrictions on beef, pork, steel and uranium exports will be removed or avoided."

The trade problem between Canada and the United States was never tariffs. In some cases and in earlier years, tariffs were significant, but even before the FTA about 70 per cent of goods travelled tariff-free between Canada and the U.S. and the remaining tariffs tended usually to be less than the currency differences. The problem was non-tariff regulations, a whole panoply of trade remedies that the Americans could enact to exclude imports into the American market. So-called antidumping regulations constitute one category of these remedies.

Under its classical definition, dumping occurs when a country exports a commodity for sale at a price cheaper than what it sells for on the domestic market. Even this definition sticks in the craw of a true believer in free trade. After all, the free market allows for loss leaders. Furthermore, in the case of steel, which is rarely an end product but is instead mostly a component of another commodity such as an automobile or appliance, any country that would engage in dumping is actually forcing a higher price structure on its products and hampering its own ability to compete in domestic and export markets.

But the United States does not rest content with the classical definition of dumping. It also uses an even vaguer criterion based on markup and profit. That is, the United States believes it has a right to, and can, enforce its notions of what a fair profit is and is not — another assault on the free market. In this case, it seems that an 8 per cent net profit should be built into the price of steel; otherwise it is considered "dumping." It would be hard to imagine any major steel company on either side of the border making an 8 per cent profit. The jewels in the crown of Canada's industry, Dofasco and Stelco, are bleeding money (we won't even talk about Algoma in Sault Sainte-Marie or Sydney Steel in Cape Breton). Bankruptcy is being freely predicted, and a 1992 headline in the *Financial Times* even welcomed the prospect: "A trip to the bankruptcy court may be just the tonic for an ailing industry."[10]

Thus, the first problem the Canadian steel industry has is that it is, in fact, the Canadian steel industry. By contrast, as we noted, there is no such thing as the Canadian automobile industry: there are Canadian plants that produce and assemble American automobiles. It is hardly likely that General Motors would complain to the American government that one of its Canadian plants is dumping Pontiacs onto the American market. The Canadian steel industry has been calling for a sectoral agreement with the United States along the lines of the agreement allegedly in place with the Auto Pact. The Americans believe this is a rather silly idea in that it opens up the American market to Canadian competition. Competition is wonderful if you own all the competitors. General Motors can sing the praises of free and open competition while pitting one plant against the other. For the American steel industry, free trade with Canada in steel means competition with competitors it doesn't own and it wants none of it.

The traditional efficiency of the Canadian steel industry has made it able not only to control the Canadian market but also to compete in the American and world markets. Until recently Canada has sold almost twice as much steel in the United States as the Americans have sold in Canada. The American market is significant to Canadian producers — about 15 per cent of Dofasco's production is sold in the U.S., and the natural market for Algoma was the American Midwest. But on an overall basis, even in the halcyon days, Canada had a scant 4 per cent of the American market.

In a recession one can argue, as the American industry obviously did, that even that's too much. But the issue goes somewhat further, and the Americans have every right to be concerned. If Canadian goods can travel freely across the border, what is to stop a Canadian steel company from buying cheap offshore steel, integrating it into another product and selling that finished product into the United States market? True, there exist all sorts of regulations concerning national origins, but how are these to be enforced effectively? After all, a similar process occurs when an automobile component firm operating on both sides of the Mexican-American border produces a part in both the U.S. and Mexico. In a pre-NAFTA version of informal North American free trade, the part is then either shipped duty-free to an assembly plant in Canada or incorporated into an automobile that enters Canada duty-free.

What if the Canadians were to set up joint ventures with steel or any other manufacturers or producers who would thus use Canada as a platform for entry into the American market? Under the terms of the current FTA, content requirements are deliberately vague in the case of exports into the United States, and the Americans can interpret them in any manner they see fit to disallow this practice.

This is the point the Americans have made to Canada over the Honda and Volkswagen as well as with magnesium producer Norsk Hydro in Quebec. When the Canadian government presented the FTA as a trade liberalization measure, it was either lying to its own citizens and the Europeans and Japanese or didn't understand the treaty it was signing. There seems to be evidence on both sides. In their book *Faith and Fear*, Bruce Doern and Brian Tomlin point out that Canada's main goal in the negotiations was to spell out rules concerning subsidies, countervail and dumping, but it was unable to do so.[11] Ironically, the authors conclude that Canada's failure may have saved the treaty because the tradeoffs required to reach any possible agreements with the Americans would have broken the pro-free trade alliance in Canada. A case in point seems to be steel, where the major corporations promoted the agreement on the assurances that their export positions would be protected. While it may be too strong to suggest that the steel industry was sabotaged in that final negotiating session on October 3, 1987, it was certainly sacrificed because the United States made it perfectly clear that Congress would never give up any of its jurisdiction over trade matters. Giving up sovereignty was for other countries.

With NAFTA and its complex but very exclusionary rules of origin, even the pretence of trade liberalization has been given up. The United States has made it quite clear that neither Canada nor Mexico will be export platforms for the Japanese or Europeans into the American market.

Content regulations rule out virtually any joint ventures between a Canadian and non-American firm with any hope of entering the American market. If an industry is not wholly owned by American parents, or virtually so, Canadian exports face the same countervail sanctions as any other country. This is what is called free trade. As one columnist put it, there is a "message to Canadian producers from the Americans: don't get good at it."[12]

But the restrictions on entering the American market are not only economic or primarily economic, and being an American-owned company does not provide automatic exemption. Giles Gherson wrote about the price differential between American and Canadian sugar, which gave bakery and confectionery producers in Canada a decided edge over American producers.[13] During and after the FTA negotiations, the American government made several moves under different pretexts to restrict the entry of Canadian sugar into the U.S. The net has been cast ever wider to include cocoa and sugar manufactured in Canada from foreign sources, flavoured syrup, pancake mixes: virtually any product that contains sugar is being targeted. And the message is given to conglomerates such as Kraft, General Foods and Nestlé to be very careful about their Canadian operations: "Genuine doubts that they would be able to ship their products unhindered into the U.S. can only discourage food companies from investing further in Canadian plants. Welcome to free trade, U.S. style."

From his rampart in ultraright field, the Toronto *Globe and Mail*'s Terence Corcoran allows that the FTA and NAFTA do not "go far enough" in removing trade frictions.[14] He quotes two strategies to solve the problem. One comes from steel analyst Jay Gordon, who believes that the current dumping wars threaten the very existence of the Canadian steel industry. In Gordon's view, a plea for compassion should be issued on the grounds that the destruction of the Canadian steel industry would adversely affect American corporations and interests: "In many respects, damaging the Canadian economy is no different than damaging the New York economy or the California economy." Corcoran then quotes Michael Trebilcock, coauthor of *Unfinished Business: Reforming Trade Remedy Laws in North America*, who notes that the vague stopgap mandate of the dispute settlement mechanism of the FTA has been weakened even further in NAFTA with a trilateral commission that "will consider issues concerning the relationship between competition laws and policies in the free trade area." Trebilcock wants Canada to get tough and demand a side agreement to finish the unfinished business of dumping and subsidies.

The Americans have already made it quite clear that they have no intention of binding themselves to an international treaty that weakens the constitutional rights and duties of the U.S. Congress. Meanwhile, by signing the FTA and NAFTA, Canada has made it quite clear that it accepts the American position. So, where is the basis for a side deal?

And as for Gordon's idea of trying to convince the Americans that damaging the Canadian economy is no different from damaging the American, what if the United States were to agree?

Air Transport: Horse and Rabbit Stew

Nothing could symbolize Canada's retreat from the global (as opposed to continental) trading system more aptly than the impending destruction of the existing Canadian air transport system. The saga of Canada's airlines puts one in mind of the old Agatha Christie novel *And Then There Were None* — except that in this version, the hero and heroine do not escape the killer. The outcome is seemingly inevitable and known well in advance of the dénouement: Air Canada and Canadian Airlines International will go either jointly or separately into the maw of either one or two U.S. carriers. Only the process by which this will happen is a mystery as this is written in June 1993, with many bumps and slumps and twists and turns still to come.

Each episode brings odd and hitherto unexpected developments. Money-making reservations systems become more important than the money-losing aircraft on which seats are being reserved or the countries whose flags they fly. The president of American Airlines muses about abandoning the airline business altogether. At the same time, he offers to take control (but not really control) of near-bankrupt Canadian Airlines, without even taking the trouble of borrowing enough money to buy all of it. (Just consider where the North American economy would be if Michael Milken had figured that one out: Robert Campeau would be alive and well and even the Reichmanns would be chirping like canaries.) And there is more to come, as money-bleeding Air Canada sells assets to buy a minority position in bankrupt Continental Airlines — not the first choice, but British Airways beat Air Canada to the punch with a partial buyout of USAir, which is only potentially bankrupt.

It used to be one of the jokes of the decolonizing period of the 1950s and 1960s that a newly independent country needed a flag, an anthem and an airline if it was to be taken seriously. There was an element of vanity involved, but new countries also saw the need to establish their own ties with their neighbours and have their own direct access to world capitals. An airline is as much a part of the transport and communications system as a highway. For Canada, the internal and external airline route system is as necessary today as the transcontinental rail system was a hundred years ago. What would Canada look like, and how would it have developed, if its urban and regional centres were not linked directly but merely existed as spurs off the U.S. continental system?

Canada's aviation pioneers were First World War flying aces such as Billy Bishop and bush pilots such as Grant McConachie. The bush pilots, who proved that there was no practical alternative to aircraft if the north was to be integrated into Canada, held the first Canadian "northern vision." By the late 1920s the federal government was subsidizing some early aerial surveys and inaugurating an air mail service, but the Depression forced a halt. In Prime Minister R.B. Bennett's eyes it was an unseemly frill for airplanes to fly the mail "while desperate prairie farmers, listening below, could hear the planes flying through skies blackened with the blowing dust of their drought-ruined farms."

Bennett had other considerations. His experience with the railways taught him that there must be some form of public control over the building and operation of a civil air system that would both prevent overbuilding and ensure that national interests were served in an east-west linkage. The more profitable prospect of developing north-south feeder lines to the U.S. transcontinental system had to be resisted. Manitoba grain baron James Richardson, along with executives of both the CPR and the CNR, had already invested in a commercial airline that was operating in various parts of the country. Bennett gave him no encouragement.

When Bennett was defeated in 1935, C.D. Howe became minister in the new transport department, which took over responsibility for civil aviation from the defence department. Howe recognized that the small population base, vast distances and natural north-south pull made public participation or at least oversight necessary in the development of an east-west air transport system just as in the development of the railways — and that a single airline must have a monopoly on profitable routes to subsidize service to the smaller or more remote centres. Although he was a free enterpriser if ever one lived, Howe was particularly adamant about maintaining Trans-Canada Airlines as a government monopoly. It wasn't until 1949 that Ottawa grudgingly allowed privately held Canadian Pacific Airlines to fly the initially money-losing routes across the Pacific.

Canada has had a fundamental difficulty with state-owned corporations. Sometimes they were established to fill a void created by a reluctant private sector, or as a solution to problems created by that sector. In other instances the goal was to resolve a genuine conflict between the public and private interest. Most often, however, Crown corporations were established to facilitate the private market system. Thus they owe their existence to a system and a governmental structure that are ideologically hostile to them. The result is that they are usually on borrowed time.

The first stage in destroying Crown corporations is to eliminate the sense of public purpose that brought them into existence. Once this is done, the rationale for selling them is in place. The process often blows up in our faces — Petro-Canada and De Havilland being examples in the recent past, and the privatization of Ontario Hydro being one that may be about to happen.

In the 1970s Trans-Canada Airlines, by then renamed Air Canada, was a successful flag carrier. It was also bloated and inefficient, and was even the subject of an inquiry into its financial management. In 1978 its mandate was changed: it was instructed to operate as any commercial airline would. It later began to eliminate service on some unprofitable routes and to replace many of its jet services with slower propeller planes operated by affiliated companies, just as was happening in the newly deregulated skies south of the border. Describing this change in mandate a few years later, Toronto *Globe and Mail* columnist Jeffrey Simpson wrote, "What public service does Air Canada now fulfil? The answer is none." If it didn't fulfil a public purpose, the logical answer was to sell it.

Despite all attempts to be lean and mean and profitable, Air Canada showed a loss in 1981. The next part of the privatization scenario now comes into play. If the corporation no longer serves a public purpose and can't even be counted on to show a profit, selling it is no longer an ideological issue but a practical business decision. One leadership aspirant at the 1983 Tory convention received rapturous applause when he began his convention speech: "Goodbye Air Canada, farewell CBC."

In an offhand remark early in his mandate, Brian Mulroney at his exuberant best enthused that "Canada needs a national airline" and squelched rumours that Air Canada was for sale. But Air Canada needed, or thought it needed, an infusion of capital to upgrade and expand its fleet of aircraft to become a more serious international carrier as well as to handle growing competition in Canada's already saturated domestic market. If the airline wasn't going to be sold, then its capital requirements would have to come, as they always had, from government.

The Economic Council of Canada supported privatization, arguing that the airline "may not be sufficiently flexible under government ownership to adapt to stronger competitive pressures under deregulation." Privatization, it also stated, "will not lead to the sacrifice of important public policy objectives. The primary loss would be felt by those who place a high value on the symbol of a government-owned airline." In the face of this, little attention was paid to polls indicating that the majority of Canadians wanted to maintain this "symbol."

In April 1988 the government announced it would indeed be selling Air Canada, and top management was ecstatic. Air Canada filed its prospectus for the first of two tranches in September with shares sold at $8 each; the second tranche followed ten months later at $12 a share. Both issues sold briskly, with foreign investors, mostly Americans, snapping up the 25 per cent of shares non-Canadians were allowed by law to hold. But this still raised only a fraction of what the company estimated it would need for growth and modernization in the 1990s. In a dizzy rollercoaster ride, Air Canada shares soared as high as $14.83; in early 1993 they would plummet as low as $2.20.

Meanwhile, a regional carrier called Pacific Western Airlines, which had briefly been owned by the Alberta government but was newly privatized, went on a Campeauesque buying spree. In 1986 it acquired the much bigger Canadian Pacific Airlines, which in turn had recently swallowed Nordair and Eastern Provincial Airlines. The resulting company was christened Canadian Airlines International, and in 1989 it overpaid heavily to buy a faltering competitor, Wardair.

By 1990 it was clear something was going terribly wrong. That year the world's airlines lost US$2.7 billion, according to *Fortune*, and much worse was in store. Air Canada's board of directors got cold feet over president Pierre Jeanniot's ambitious growth plans and called them off. Jeanniot, after almost thirty years with the company, left abruptly. The airline's chair, Claude Taylor, assumed operating control and began to slash away, cutting 3,000 jobs and cancelling several overseas routes.

Canadian Airlines also cut jobs and routes, but losses at both companies kept swelling, approaching a combined $2 million a day by late 1992. Air Canada had enough assets to keep going on its own, but heavily leveraged Canadian suspended payments to creditors and demanded federal and provincial loan guarantees to avoid bankruptcy (guarantees that were pledged just weeks after the report of the Royal Commission on National Passenger Transportation insisted that market forces should prevail). Canadian did talk merger with Air Canada more than once, but discussions ended when it became obvious that a combined entity would carry too heavy a debt load to fly. Canadian went bouncing towards the altar with American Airlines, and the National Transportation Agency gave its consent. However, American insisted Canadian join its Sabre reservations system, without which any deal was off. It was not clear how Canadian could buy its way out of a long-term contract with the Gemini reservations system, in which it and Air Canada each held a one-third share (with the rest held by a sister company of United Airlines, an ally of Air Canada and archrival of American).

Meanwhile, the Canadian and U.S. governments were negotiating an "Open Skies" agreement that would eliminate most restrictions on transborder air traffic, although access to gates and slots at busier airports remained a sticking point. Air services had specifically been excluded from the scope of both the original Free Trade Agreement and NAFTA; the rationale was that this would be covered by separate deals, yet another example of the way the airline industry is treated differently from most other economic sectors. This special treatment, a worldwide phenomenon, has not prevented shakeouts, mergers and alliances from continuing in an industry where, in 1992, the scourge of heavy losses spread even to Japan Airlines.

In the U.S. only the top three carriers (American, United and Delta, all running big losses) plus profitable niche carrier Southwest Airlines had solid balance sheets. The next rung of carriers (Northwest, Continental and USAir) were in various stages of financial decay and had all been bought into by foreign equity partners (KLM, Air Canada and British Airways respectively), while Trans World and America West appeared to be on their deathbeds. In Europe, merger talks between British Airways and KLM broke off, but KLM did sign letters of intent with SAS, Swissair and Austrian Airlines. Air France went on a rampage, buying control of French rival UTA, domestic carrier Air Inter, Belgium's Sabena and the Czech Republic's CSA. British Airways, having already swallowed British Caledonian, bought into USAir, TAT of France and Qantas of Australia (which in turn was about to absorb domestic carrier Australian Airlines). Iberia of Spain turned its attention to private or newly privatized airlines in Argentina, Venezuela and Chile, while Aeromexico bought control of domestic rival Mexicana and AeroPeru. Though it is true that one cannot really tell the players any more without a program, it is also true that there are going to be fewer and fewer players as the game goes on.

Here in Canada, a straight merger of Air Canada and Canadian would have been unlikely to fly even had financial conditions been more favourable and capacity not quite as excessive. The red herring of competition swam frequently into view: here were two companies offering products as similar as Coke and Pepsi on domestic routes and charging identical fares, and yet according to the competition argument this duopoly was essential for travellers to have a choice. A more heretical view holds that a single dominant carrier would chop overcapacity to make itself more profitable, leaving more room for real competitors to nibble around the edges and making the disappearance of such airlines as City Express, Intair and Nationair somewhat less inevitable.

Be that as it may, the real problem is political: Air Canada has lobbied fiercely for its concept of a single international flag carrier for Canada. For this to happen, Canadian Airlines would have either to be swallowed whole or broken into pieces, with the juicy overseas morsels parcelled out to Air Canada. Any government that allowed this would risk political extermination in the west, where Canadian has its head office (Calgary) and chief maintenance base (Vancouver) — and the fallout would be as much about symbols as about jobs. But if a Canadian-American Airlines combination proved too powerful and Air Canada got pushed into oblivion, there would be howls of outrage (and worse) in Montreal, where the government gave very specific guarantees about employment levels and head office location when Air Canada was privatized. The government is not exactly looking here at a win-win situation. A domestic merger means big job losses — and vote losses. But action to prevent a merger would weaken both potential partners and lead to bankruptcy or separate mergers.

Talk of a made-in-Canada solution from Hollis Harris, late of Delta and Continental and now Air Canada's chair and president, is naïve on the face of it and downright deceptive in reality. It was Harris, after all, who signed a marketing deal with United Airlines and marketing and equity arrangements with Continental. Even a merged Canadian carrier would in all likelihood have to form a tight alliance with one of the dominant U.S. carriers. Since the U.S. partner would be several times bigger, it is evident where effective control of joint operations would lie. Moreover, the end of the longstanding airline duopoly in Canada would lead to increased pressures for U.S. and other foreign carriers to get cabotage rights to compete on domestic routes in Canada, which could mean that after a few years there would be no dominant Canadian carrier even within Canada.

Robert Crandall, the president of American Airlines, has proposed that "instead of focusing on carriers one by one, we ought to be thinking more of how the airlines of both countries can be part of the growing network of worldwide airlines." This makes sense in the new context. Both major Canadian carriers have had a difficult time competing with Americans for cross-border traffic. The existing bilateral agreement gives U.S. carriers, as a group, direct access to almost every big city in Canada, while Canadian carriers can fly to only a handful of U.S. cities. Thus somebody going, say, from Toronto to Atlanta or from Vancouver to Denver has to go all or most of the way on a U.S. carrier.

But competing toe to toe in an open, deregulated market is unlikely to be profitable for a Canadian carrier trying to operate independently. This has become painfully clear as the federal government's strategy for a new U.S.-Canada bilateral air services treaty — the so-called Open Skies negotiations — continues to unravel. The report of a federal task force noted that the only way deregulated air traffic would not be a total disaster for Canadian carriers would be for them to be given preferred access to the most popular and overcrowded terminals in the U.S. along with cabotage rights. To nobody's surprise, the Americans have rejected such proposals. But if no deals are struck and the status quo remains, the economies of scale and other price and tax advantages of the American lines come into full play, and they will continue to treat Canadian cities as mere feeders to their various hubs around the U.S.

With all other potential solutions having led to dead ends, American Airlines appeared set at the time of writing to buy a 33 per cent equity interest and 25 per cent of voting rights in Canadian Airlines. American is the biggest and most aggressive of U.S. airlines and has been described by one writer as the "pit bull of U.S. carriers." Its US$11.7 billion revenues in 1992 contrast with Canadian's C$2.8 billion. Employees have referred to Crandall variously as Fang, Darth Vader and Attila the Hun. Toronto *Globe and Mail* transport reporter Geoffrey Rowan wrote that insiders described negotiating sessions between Crandall and Canadian Airlines boss Rhys Eyton as confrontations between Godzilla and Bambi. Godzilla is unlikely to accept the notion that 33 per cent ownership doesn't give him something approaching control. American's offer of US$190 million for a one-third stake in Canadian is an interesting deal when compared with the $150 million the company paid earlier for a single route from Seattle to Tokyo.

If all goes according to plan, the two route networks would be reorganized on a continental basis. Toronto, where both are major tenants in glitzy new Terminal 3, would effectively become an American Airlines hub, and the border would become a dead letter. Canadian's routes between Vancouver and Asia are among its more tantalizing assets. If these fall under the effective control of American, access to most of the Pacific Rim would be denied to any carrier controlled in Canada. This in itself would be no great tragedy, provided that Adam Smith's invisible hand sees to it that the ability to get from here to there is not impaired. It is this ability that is vitally important, especially for the "here."

Without a solid transport grid linking Canadian cities with one another and with fast-growing regions abroad, the country would stagnate as an economic backwater. In the U.S., being a regional hub for a major airline has added enormous economic vitality to certain cities, so much so that the state of Minnesota pledged vast grants to Northwest Airlines to help maintain Minneapolis-St. Paul as a main hub. Atlanta was once the busiest railway junction in the southeastern U.S. and is now the busiest airline hub. The joke still goes that you can't get to heaven without changing planes (it used to be trains) in Atlanta. It may be a chicken-and-egg argument, but Atlanta's domination of transport helps make it the region's key economic and commercial centre.

It is perhaps worth noting that the highway system tends to relate more realistically to the flow of the continental economy, which is one reason among several that trucks have displaced a large part of rail traffic. This, incidentally, has not helped the Canadian trucking industry, which is being wiped out by U.S. competition. But it does explain Canadian National's decision to invest in a new tunnel at Sarnia to carry double-stack containers to and from the U.S. At the same time, Canadian Pacific, fresh from its acquisition of the Delaware and Hudson Railway connecting Montreal with New York State and Pennsylvania, is preparing to abandon the vestiges of its Maritimes service. Both railway companies are paying less attention to their east-west links and concentrating on U.S. traffic.

So a merger of the two countries' transportation systems appears to be well under way. But they don't exactly merge. During the First World War, army field kitchens used to prepare a dish called "horse and rabbit stew." It was made of equal parts horse and rabbit — one horse to one rabbit. This is very much analogous to the Canada-U.S. Free Trade Agreement, along with ancillary arrangements such as the one emerging in the airline industry. Canada has not so much entered into a joint venture as it has integrated itself into the ten-times-larger U.S. economy. Southern Ontario in particular needs direct access to the market it has been integrated into. It may not matter all that much where control of the airline industry is exercised if planes are flying where people want to go and fares are not too exorbitant. The lines of commerce, and therefore of airline traffic, are running increasingly north and south rather than east and west. The old premise on which Canada's airlines, railways and pipelines were built may exist no longer.

Of course, if fares or schedules or service standards fail to satisfy air travellers in Canada, a Canadian government will find itself under pressure to act. It may even find itself in circumstances similar to the ones that led to the creation of Trans-Canada Airlines in the first place. There is no sign, however, that the sense of public purpose that underlay the policies of both R.B. Bennett and C.D. Howe in the 1930s could be recaptured by any conceivable Canadian government in the 1990s.

Agriculture: Trade Policy or Social Policy?

As we have noted, the absence of any clear definition of what constitutes a subsidy is one of the more nettlesome aspects of trade agreements in general, and of NAFTA in particular. This can play havoc with enforcement of trade rules and leaves the way open to all manner of mischief. Depending which side of the fence you inhabit, anything that benefits your neighbour can be construed as an unfair subsidy that violates the most basic market principles, while of course the benefits that flow your way are just part of the natural order of things.

This is true in all sorts of industrial sectors, but it is especially true in agriculture. Thus American hog farmers, annoyed by competition in their home market from lower-priced Canadian hogs, could make the straight-faced assertion that supply stabilization programs in Canada constituted a government subsidy. Once the U.S. farm lobbyists got to work, this came to warrant punishment in the form of countervailing duties, that most arbitrary of trade barriers and the easiest to invoke. They fought hard, though ultimately in vain, to obstruct imports into the U.S. of one of the few farm commodities in which Canada appeared to have a competitive advantage.

The bilateral dispute panel set up under the FTA ruled that, contrary to the assertions of the plaintiffs, Canada's hog stabilization program performed a regulatory function and did not constitute a subsidy scheme. This episode, which reached its dénouement in 1992, provided rhetorical ammunition for both pro- and anti-free-traders: the dispute panel ruled in Canada's favour and showed it could be effective in resolving trade conflicts, but on the other hand the FTA clearly lacked the teeth to prevent such trade disruptions from arising in the first place and to dispel doubts about the promised access to U.S. markets that was the agreement's main selling point.

Of course, the dispute panel heard little about the hefty benefits conferred on American ranchers who are asked to pay a mere pittance for grazing rights on public lands in the western plains. When Bill Clinton later tried to correct this with a proposal to raise grazing fees and help narrow his federal budget deficit, he met a wall of resistance and had to perform one of his many humiliating back-pedalling acts. Nor was much said about the prosperous landowners in California's semiarid San Joaquin Valley who grow monsoon crops such as rice and can afford to raise thirsty alfalfa crops to feed their dairy cattle because irrigation water from the bounteous federal teat is priced so cheaply. Subsidies, you say? Not in the eyes of the big corporate farmers who benefit so handsomely. And not in the eyes of their friends in Washington.

Farmers have powerful lobbies in most Western capitals, even though this sometimes seems superfluous. Farmers themselves are often their own best lobbyists. Even where farms are owned and managed by big faceless corporations, the cherubic faces of the traditional farm family can provide a useful mask in any public relations exercise. Around the world, farmers hold a strong grip on public perceptions, and in richer countries on the public purse as well. A well-timed demonstration by angry farmers can influence public policy far more effectively than millions spent prowling legislative corridors.

The family farm is, in any case, more than a mask. Farming in Canada is still dominated by independent family-owned units to an extent virtually unknown in any other part of the economy. In other sectors, thousands of family-owned businesses have succumbed to larger corporate entities with their stronger financial and technical support and their greater economies of scale. Many farmers, like many small retailers and restaurateurs, are able to hang on to what they have only through inhumanly long work hours, underpaid jobs by family members and sheer determination. If large corporations have often resisted the urge to rush into agriculture, it may have much to do with poor rates of return on capital.

Because many farmers even in rich countries lead a difficult and precarious existence — and because they grow most of what we eat — it is only natural to find sympathy with many of their concerns. Canada's struggling farmers are not cheered by some of the changes that may lie ahead because of evolving world trade regimes. Some of the hidden and not-so-hidden subsidies and supports they rely on may not be around a whole lot longer, and a way of life is at risk.

Despite some unfriendly stereotypes about rural conservatism, farmers actually have a head start over industrial workers in adjusting to change. In Canada and other countries their numbers have fallen dramatically over the decades while those who remain have achieved great leaps in productivity under often hostile conditions. Unfortunately, in an era in which the world is moving towards ever more relentless competition, not even this is enough to assure a promising future.

Government farm policies in different parts of the world sometimes seem aimed at achieving exactly the opposite of what the public interest would dictate. In the wealthy countries of Western Europe, farmers are cosseted with generous subsidies and import protection that encourages them to produce far more food than consumers are willing and able to pay for. The result is high prices for consumers as this surplus production is kept away from local markets, higher taxes for everyone, and mountainous surpluses that play havoc with farm incomes when they are dumped abroad. In 1991 EC farm subsidies reached US$83 billion and accounted for one-third of the Community budget.[15] Much of this was used to flood world markets with wheat and other commodities that could have been grown more cheaply in such places as Australia and Argentina, where farmers get along virtually without subsidies, or in struggling Eastern European countries looking desperately for export markets.

A common line among food exporters, of course, is that everyone else subsidizes farmers so we'll do it just to stay competitive. Canada and the United States have been no slouches at this game. In fact, OECD figures suggest that Canadian farmers depend on government support for almost as high a proportion of their incomes as farmers in the European Community. And that's not all: Canada is a member of the Cairns group of countries, which has urged an end to farm subsidies; this pose might seem less duplicitous if Canada's own practices were in keeping with what it preaches. (The world champion subsidizers are the Swiss and the Scandinavians. The OECD found that Swiss farmers received four francs in public support for every franc paid by actual buyers.)

But in much of Africa and some other places where food is in short supply or beyond the reach of large numbers of people, exactly the reverse occurs: bureaucrats and politicians worried about their urban constituencies dictate, or attempt to dictate, artificially low food prices. This keeps farm incomes low and provides little incentive for farmers to increase production and meet local or regional needs. The result is continuing shortages and a population shift towards urban areas that are ill-equipped to receive new migrants. "Gifts" of surplus food from abroad sometimes just worsen the situation. It would seem that rich countries should be producing less food and poor countries can and should be producing more, but misguided policies on both sides keep this from happening.

As we write, the countries of Europe and North America appear to be running the very real risk of a trade war over farm subsidies. The French government has been particularly unapologetic in its defence of EC farm policies, and it doubtless has the silent support of some EC partners who are more than happy to have France take the heat. Economic considerations play only a small part in this stance. French farmers have been noisy and creative in their protests, and political parties of both the left and the right depend on the farm vote. Farm families account for less than 5 per cent of the French population, but their political and social influence is huge. In earlier times France was slower to industrialize than Britain or Germany; at the end of the Second World War half the population still lived in the countryside. Many urban dwellers continue to identify with their country cousins, and there is a pervasive sense that the countryside represents the real France, *la France profonde*. This sentiment is not to be trifled with.

France and its European neighbours are hardly alone. The Japanese are conspicuous in their reverence for farmers and seem willing to put up with politicians who maintain a blanket ban on rice imports and thus force all Japanese to pay several times the world price for their daily rice. South Korea, with its dramatic population shift from country to city in the last three decades, seems poised for a wave of rural nostalgia that could place farmers on a higher pedestal, with serious implications for trade policy. And as we noted, even in hard-nosed North America the tendency to romanticize farming —

which accounts directly for less than 2 per cent of employment but for a whole lot more in political terms — persists.

Some parts of Canadian agriculture could survive and indeed flourish in an unprotected world trade environment, but others would suffer a high fatality rate even with generous adjustment programs. Although Canada's supply management programs in milk, eggs and poultry remained largely untouched in the early years of so-called free trade with the U.S., there was growing pressure from the GATT to dismantle farm quotas and replace them with a system of external tariffs. Supply management assures steady supply and steady prices, but some of these prices are higher than they need be. This hurts consumers and hobbles exports of processed foods, with resulting job losses. Quota holders under supply management systems are sheltered from serious competition and have little incentive to reduce costs or improve quality.

Parallels can be found in several parts of the world. We mentioned the Japanese ban on rice imports: an open market would devastate Japan's culturally pleasing but generally inefficient agriculture. Many farmers in the U.S. and Europe are big growers of sugar beet, surely one of the world's more nonsensical crops since it costs so much more to produce than sugar cane. Their governments have created elaborate quota systems that deprive cane-producing countries of much needed export income and foster a big market in intermediate-priced substitutes such as corn-based sweeteners. Since Canada has not allowed its sugar import policies to be dictated by beet growers, Canadian confectionery makers pay less for their most basic raw material than their U.S. competitors and thus — surprise — find themselves threatened occasionally with countervailing duties. But by the same token, Canadians have imposed on themselves an artificially created comparative disadvantage in exports of processed foods containing supply-managed ingredients.

Agriculture has gone through many shakeouts, and the worst may be yet to come. The U.S.-Canada Free Trade Agreement exempted supply-managed goods from its provisions, but it is hard to believe these exemptions are permanent; a future round of multilateral trade talks could wipe them out even if NAFTA doesn't. Nor can taxpayer support for grain farmers be taken for granted. Even some growers who boast of their high productivity could find out the hard way what self-reliance really means (although a simultaneous removal of European subsidies could do wonders for world grain prices).

It would not be pretty to see thousands more Canadian farmers pushed out of business or "for sale" signs saturating the countryside even more than they do now, and it does not have to happen. Even if some of the economic arguments look precarious, there are strong social arguments in favour of a vibrant rural life. If Switzerland dutifully subsidizes its farmers to the tune of billions of francs each year, it is not because the Swiss are blind to economic reality but rather because they want to keep the countryside populated; it is a way of preserving valuable cultural traditions and exalting the national soul (if such a term can be used in the Swiss context). Norway and Finland, where high latitudes, short growing seasons and mediocre soils would seem to militate against commercial agriculture, are also big farm subsidizers. Besides the cultural arguments, there have been military reasons for maintaining a strong rural population base — Norway's long, vulnerable coastline and Finland's sometimes uneasy coexistence with its powerful Russian neighbour.

Rationales such as these are hardly foreign to Canadian thinking. Federal transfer payments keep the Atlantic region from losing yet more of its population, and government outlays allow northern residents to live in comfort despite a weak economic base. Here are instances where strict economic logic has ceded to social and occasionally even military considerations, and in neither case have foreign trade sanctions been invoked. These subsidies have gone to entire regions rather than to specific products or producers, and so far this falls within the guidelines of multilateral trade rules.

It may be time, however, for Canadians to draw a clearer distinction between trade policy and social policy. Trade policy is probably not an ideal tool for achieving social policy goals because this can create friction with foreign trading partners and, of more direct impact, because it means higher prices and thus reduced economic activity for Canadians. But abandoning trade policy as a social tool does not mean abandoning social policy goals, unless a particular government is looking for an excuse to do precisely that. Rather, it means finding different tools, some of which may not be justifiable in strict economic terms. Social arguments in some cases may be strong enough to overcome economic logic. But it is important to draw the distinction and to recognize what is being done for economic purposes and what is being done for social purposes rather than trying to pretend that every socially motivated program brings a net economic benefit. If a government adopts certain anti-economic policies in the name of a higher goal, this should be spelled out clearly so that the country can see where it is going.

In the case of agriculture, governments traditionally have supported farm products with subsidies and quotas, in effect underwriting business losses and creating a vast welfare scheme. But it may make more sense to provide guarantees of support for farm families themselves rather than for what they produce. That could give them the security they need to stay on the land, which many Canadians see as an important goal, and to help them find ways to diversify their incomes. Farmers would then be inclined to produce only what they could sell, production and prices would find more satisfactory levels, fertilizer and pesticide use might fall, corporate farm owners would not be siphoning vast amounts of public funds, and the cost to taxpayers could drop substantially.

In a more liberal world trade environment, many Canadian farmers can thrive on their own and break away from any lingering dependency on government handouts. Others may be less fortunate and could require some new form of assistance if they are to remain on the farm. We readily admit we have not worked out the details of how any such scheme might work, nor can we be sure how Canada's trade partners might react. But something better has to be found than the current international system, which has put farmers in rich countries on a glorified form of welfare without any clear benefit to their self-esteem or to the interests of consumers and taxpayers and with clear detriment to the economies of poorer parts of the world.

Chapter 7

Culture, Identity and the Nation-State

Globalization is generally conceived of primarily in economic terms, and so far in this book we have dealt primarily with economic issues. After all, it is economic institutions — multinational corporations and banks — that have been the chief promoter of the global idea. It is in the economic sphere that the borders of the nation-state have been most palpably weakened through the activities of these institutions and through the growth of trading blocs. It is in their economic lives, through declining employment in some places and growth in others, that people have felt the effects of globalization most directly.

And yet globalization is far from being solely an economic phenomenon. It is not necessary to be a strict Marxist-Leninist to see a connection between economic developments on the one hand and the evolution of people's culture and identity on the other. This is especially true in that globalization is affecting areas of the economy, such as communications, that are intimately connected to culture. The overall effect of these changes is to weaken the relationship between people's culture and identity and the nation-state in which they live. Again, it is not hard to see that if a combination of ideology, fiscal weakness and transborder economic integration reduces the role that the nation-state plays in people's economic and political lives, the effects will be felt on some level in their cultural lives as well. Cultural changes are by their nature more difficult to pin down than economic ones, and these changes, being in their early stages, are especially so. But the politics of culture and identity have been exceptionally volatile recently, and it is useful to try to understand this volatility as part of a larger picture.

Jihad and McWorld

In the modern era, people's culture and identity have been largely — although not completely, despite the totalitarian claims of the nation-state on people's loyalty — encompassed within the borders of a particular state. The French live in France, the Italians in Italy, the Canadians in Canada. Being French or Italian or Canadian connects people to a particular history, particular symbols, even, it is sometimes claimed, particular values. Other levels of identity — ethnic, regional, religious — have always been in competition with the ones defined by states. One obvious response to the weakening of the nation-state is for these levels of identity to assert themselves more strongly. As we noted in chapter four, there is no contradiction between this development and the tendency towards larger units manifested in the growth of trading blocs and global corporations. What is operating here is a kind of Law of the Excluded Middle, the middle in this case being the nation-state. "To be a Welsh European," writes Jan Morris, "is my *own* political ambition, and the object of my patriotism is a Wales with its own seat on what Thomas Jefferson, himself a Welshman, would certainly have called a Continental Congress."[1] There appears to be little room in her schema for the United Kingdom of Great Britain and Northern Ireland.

For some observers, the exclusion of the middle is a highly disturbing development. In this view, the nation-state provided a medium, however imperfect, for democratic self-determination. Take it away and you are left with warring tribes on the one hand and homogenized blandness on the other — in the memorable phrase of Benjamin R. Barber, Jihad vs. McWorld.[2] "Just beyond the horizon of current events lie two possible political futures — both bleak, neither democratic," writes Barber. "The first is a retribalization of large swaths of humankind by war and bloodshed. . . . The second is being borne in on us by the onrush of economic and ecological forces that demand integration and uniformity and that mesmerize the world with fast music, fast computers, and fast food." To characterize the changes in this way is, of course, to emphasize their worst aspects, but it is hard not to agree with Barber that their worst aspects are primarily what we have seen.

Still, nostalgia for the fading power of the nation-state is no more an adequate response to these political and cultural developments than it is to the corresponding economic ones. In Canada, cultural nationalists have tended to see the nation-state as an instrument of resistance to McWorld, arguing that state agencies such as the Canadian Broadcasting Corporation, the National Film Board and the Canada Council have played key roles in keeping the country distinct. However, it is equally possible to see the nation-state as an agent of McWorld.

The German writer Uwe Pörksen's nightmare vision of McWorld revolves around what he calls "plastic words."[3] Pörksen regards these words — *information, identity, development, transportation, modernization, communication* and others — as the "language of an international dictatorship," found throughout the industrialized world. It is characteristic of these words that they have long existed in the vernacular but have acquired new meanings through their association with science. The "international dictatorship" exercises its power by imposing particular ways of thinking through these words, and the nation-state, which tends to impose linguistic uniformity within its borders, has been its ally: "The nation-state weeds out languages. In this area it proves itself to be the pedlar of global unification."

The rise of levels of identity larger than those encompassed by the nation-state has not been limited to lowest-common-denominator homogenization and international thought control. It has, however, so far manifested itself primarily in the political sphere. Being a European or being a North American have always been significant cultural categories, of course, but there is not yet much evidence that economic integration has had an impact on how these categories interact with other levels of people's core identity.

What there has clearly been, however, is an increasing tendency for people who live in one state to regard what other states do as their legitimate business, regardless of traditional notions of national sovereignty and noninterference. This tendency has been most pronounced on environmental issues, where the global nature of the problems and the need for international solutions are clear (see chapter three). For Canada to ban CFCs on its own would not be of much benefit even to Canadians if other countries did not act in concert. This form of international consciousness has seeped into other issue areas as well. The international outcry about the fate of the Kurds in Iraq after the Gulf War in 1991, which George Bush would have preferred to consider an internal Iraqi matter, was a turning point in this regard.

Making it more difficult for regimes to invoke the sanctity of national sovereignty to excuse oppression is no doubt a positive development. But the idea of a code of human rights that can be applied across cultural as well as state borders raises some delicate questions. These questions landed in Canada along with Nada, a Saudi Arabian who applied to be admitted as a refugee on grounds that as a woman she was persecuted in Saudi Arabia, even though the relevant United Nations conventions did not include gender persecution among the criteria for refugee status. While there was much sympathy for her in Canada, Immigration Minister Bernard Valcourt argued in early 1993 that if Canada broadened its criteria to include gender-related persecution, it might be guilty of imperialism in imposing Canadian standards on other nations. The government eventually decided to admit Nada, and its Immigration and Refugee Board issued guidelines that could lead to the admission of other women facing gender persecution in the future, but the larger question was not addressed.

Europeans once took for granted the self-evident truth of their Christian faith and had no difficulty in justifying the imposition of Christianity on the peoples of other continents. Even many Christians have now had second thoughts about this approach and look on the history of Christian evangelization with some skepticism, but it is difficult to find a similarly skeptical view of the universal applicability of the western concept of human rights. Yet in the area of the relationship between the individual and the collectivity, and certainly in the area of the relationship between the sexes, this concept is at odds with concepts embedded in many of the world's cultures. On the one hand, it can be argued that these cultures have the right to their own autonomous development. On the other hand, the many cultures that do not allow women even the degree of freedom and equality that they have attained in the West tend to be ones whose development has been controlled almost exclusively by men.

Although some human rights NGOs have in the past been sympathetic to the idea that there is an element of cultural relativism in human rights, their attitude has been affected by the extent to which governments have perverted this idea to justify abuses of democratic and civil rights. At a regional conference on human rights in Bangkok in March 1993, in preparation for the World Conference on Human Rights in Vienna in June, Asian human rights NGOs affirmed the universal nature of human rights and the special importance of women's rights.[4] This position worked its way into the official statement of Asian governments a week later and into the declaration of the Vienna conference. Still, even if the notion of a universally applicable code of human rights is gaining ground, it is safe to say that the theoretical and practical complexities involved will keep jurists and human rights workers occupied for some time to come.

But the questions posed by McWorld and other manifestations of transnational culture and identity have so far not been as intense as those posed by Jihad. The dangers of Jihad take on their most dramatic forms in distant parts of the world: clan warfare in Somalia, ethnic cleansing in Bosnia, fighting between minorities and minorities within minorities in the republics of the former Soviet Union. The tendency to regroup into smaller units, often at odds with other small units, can be seen in the West as well. In North America, the failure of Canada's last two constitutional initiatives represents one manifestation of this tendency. Battles between African and Korean Americans on the streets of Los Angeles are another. The new intensity and intolerance surrounding struggles for group rights, especially on university campuses, are a third.

Of course, these forms of identification and the conflicts they engender have existed for generations; in many cases they are much older than the modern nation-state. To a large extent, it is precisely through suppressing these identities that the modern nation-state emerged (and, if Uwe Pörksen is correct, set the stage for its own destruction[5]). From a bloody crusade in the thirteenth century through repressive language policies, centralized administration and a uniform education system, France has endeavoured to extend the French identity developed in the heartland around Paris to the Bretons, Basques and Occitans on the periphery of what became French territory. An even more deliberate and extensive program of linguistic and cultural homogenization was undertaken in the United States, where efforts were made to imbue immigrants with American civic culture along with the English language.

For reasons of historical circumstance rather than principle, Canada was more ambivalent. Its civic culture was based on its membership in the British Empire, which has been a thin reed at least since the Second World War. Its foundational cultural duality precluded the imposition of a unitary culture on all Canadians. And the cultural force of gravity of the adjacent American giant has meant that Canadians are always subject to cultural influences from outside their borders. Ottawa's incapacity to establish even a modest degree of cultural uniformity was acknowledged and given a positive spin with the adoption of an official policy of multiculturalism in 1972.

However, the distinction between Canadian cultural plurality and the cultural uniformity of France or the United States, never as sharp as it appeared on the surface, has become even fuzzier in the last few years, which have seen a decline in the power of governments everywhere to impose an official culture on their citizens. In the United States, laments for the loss of a shared civic space (such as Arthur Schlesinger's book *The Disuniting of America*[6]) have been frequently heard. Optimists, such as writers in *The Economist*, argue that despite the current troubles the assimilative power of the American ideal will eventually triumph.[7] Pessimists rage at "politically correct" Afrocentrists and multiculturalists who are destroying America from within. Both share an assumption, possibly unwarranted, that the model of a national culture contiguous with political boundaries is still applicable in an era when those boundaries mean less than they used to.

Living with Multiple Gods

National cultures in the West were based on another assumption that is fraying at the edges: the assumption of Western cultural superiority. The muted nature of the celebration of the five hundredth anniversary of Christopher Columbus's crossing of the Atlantic in 1992 was a reflection of just how tattered that assumption has become. As little as thirty years ago, the idea that Columbus's voyage was anything other than a major step in the march of progress would have been consigned to the margins of respectable thought. Whatever doubts there might have been about Columbus's own character and motivation would not have extended to the overall enterprise that he stood for. The very name Columbus had come to represent a bold step into the unknown.

But in 1992, with Columbus in the media spotlight as a result of the quincentenary, the mood was very different. Books such as Thomas Berger's *A Long and Terrible Shadow* and Ronald Wright's *Stolen Continents*, which focused on how the last five hundred years had been experienced by people who had lived in the Americas for millennia before Columbus arrived, attracted wide and largely favourable attention.[8] University of Pennsylvania history professor Michael Zuckerman perhaps summed up the mood as well as anyone:

We see in the Columbian venture the proclivities of the West for exploitation, cultural imperialism, and incompetence in understanding other cultures or coexisting with them. With 500 years of perspective, what we might try to focus on now is an effort to overcome the cultural baggage we brought with us 500 years ago and continue to embody in our cultural life now.

The West has a singular inability to live with pluralism, to live with multiple gods. Since the fifteenth century there have been bloody struggles to impose our conception of the "true god" and an inability to accept other ways of life. We've been struggling with that in the twentieth century, but the struggle has a long way to go. It's sobering to rethink the Columbian voyage, and the trepidatious celebration of the quincentennial is one measure of that slow and painful assumption of responsibility.[9]

The Columbus anniversary became caught up in a conflict whose main battleground has been American university campuses, although it has appeared in different forms in other sectors of society and has certainly had its echoes in Canada as well. The conflict has gone by various names, being perhaps best known as "the political correctness debate" or simply "PC." More striking to Canadians, however, was the emergence of "multiculturalism" as one of the most common descriptions of what was at stake in the debate.

This was not quite multiculturalism in the Canadian sense: Ukrainians, Italians and Portuguese were not among the groups pressing for recognition of their suppressed cultures. Rather, the debate focused on efforts of African Americans, Latinos and other people with Third World origins, along with women and gays and lesbians, to break the monopoly on the cultural canon held by "dead white males." And yet at the core of American multiculturalism, as of Canadian, lay a vision of numerous cultural groups coexisting within a single political framework. In the United States, this has given rise to various forms of "identity politics," among which Afrocentrism has perhaps received the most attention.[10] At times this strain of politics leads to a kind of competitive victimology, as the strength of a group's claim for redress is directly related to where it stands in the hierarchy of historical victimization. But as has often been noted, identity politics differs from the kind of demand for redress that characterized, say, the movement for women's suffrage or later for civil rights in that it insists on the recognition of groups as groups rather than on individual equality.

Was all this a serious threat to the American ideology of cultural uniformity? It certainly touched a nerve, as the vehement and sometimes almost hysterical response to it has indicated. Thus, Shelby Steele has called identity politics the "New Sovereignty," maintaining that "in America today . . . sovereignty — that is, power to act autonomously — is bestowed upon any group that is able to construct itself around a perceived grievance."[11] And in the immediate aftermath of the Gulf War, conservative columnist George Will implicitly lumped the multiculturalists with Saddam Hussein:

> In this low-visibility, high-intensity war, [National Endowment for the Humanities chair] Lynne Cheney is secretary of domestic defense. The foreign adversaries her husband, Dick [George Bush's defense secretary], must keep at bay are less dangerous, in the long run, than the domestic forces with which she must deal. Those forces are fighting against the conservation of the common culture that is the nation's social cement. She, even more than a Supreme Court justice, deals with constitutional things. The real Constitution, which truly constitutes America, is the national mind as shaped by the intellectual legacy that gave rise to the Constitution and all the habits, mores, customs and ideas that sustain it.[12]

Will is undoubtedly correct in perceiving the cultural unity of the United States as being more fragile than it used to be, but has he identified the cause of its fragility or merely the symptoms? Is American cultural unity threatened by enemies within, or do the enemies within appear as strong as they do because the American nation-state, and with it the "national mind," have been weakened for other reasons?

People's identities are not generally simple and unitary but rather complex and layered. In composing the identity of different individuals, ancestry, geography, political allegiance, religion, gender and generation vary in their prominence and interact with one another in diverse ways. There are obvious examples. The relationship between gender and religion is not the same for a woman seeking to come to terms with the patriarchal tradition of the Roman Catholic Church or Orthodox Judaism as it is for her male coreligionists. A touchstone of the American identity such as Ellis Island will evoke one response in an American whose ancestors landed there in the 1890s, another response in one whose ancestors experienced the Middle Passage from Africa a century earlier, a different response again in one whose ancestors came from Old to New England a century before that, and still another in someone whose ancestors crossed the land bridge from Asia in the remote past. Germans born in 1950 will relate to their German identity in a different way from Germans born in 1920. In other words, most people's identity is, to some degree at least, irreducibly hyphenated.

The overall effect of the developments described here — the growth of trade blocs, the emergence of an international conscious-ness especially around environmental and human rights issues, the declining relevance of the idea of absolute national sovereignty, the proliferation of communications technologies that do not respect national borders — has been to make the situation still more complex and diminish the possibility of creating a simple, unitary identity in most parts of the world. With these developments, competition for people's allegiance has only intensified and the relative strength of nation-states in this competition has been weakened.

In addition, population movements have weakened the idea of a single national identity in most western countries by making them more ethnically diverse. About 250,000 Torontonians now report Chinese ethnic origin; almost as many report ethnic origins in the Indian subcontinent. Vancouver's much smaller population includes 179,000 people of Chinese ethnic origin.[13] In the United States, it is estimated that by 2030 about 40 per cent of the population will have ancestral roots in Africa, Asia or Latin America.[14] Liberal Party of Canada research director Chaviva Hošek, who came to Montreal from Czechoslovakia via Israel as a young girl in the 1950s, suggests that economic and cultural changes have made the rootlessness and insecurity that were her family's lot a universal experience; we are all now "permanent immigrants." In North America, whose nation-states have incorporated the idea of dealing with ethnic diversity in one way or another into the national myth, such population changes nevertheless lead to social tensions. They are even more difficult to accommodate in Western Europe, where the idea of a shared culture that has evolved over centuries plays a more central role in most countries.

To a certain extent at least, people assume a national identity — sometimes at the expense of ethnic and regional and religious iden-tities that have deeper roots — because the nation-state offers mate-rial and social rewards. Newfoundland's 1948 referendum on entering the Canadian Confederation largely revolved around ques-tions of this sort. A narrow majority of Newfoundlanders chose to value the prospect of family allowance cheques over the island's tradition of sturdy if somewhat compromised independence. Decades later spirited arguments about whether the right decision had been made could still be heard in the taverns of St. John's.[15]

Now that a combination of ideology and historical evolution has led to an erosion of the material benefits of Confederation, the context of those arguments has changed, not only in Newfoundland but also in other parts of Canada with strong regional identities. Similar and if anything even more pronounced forces in the United States have made the rewards of membership in American society neither as available nor as apparent to many people. The groups that have been advocating multiculturalism most vigorously have tended to be the ones that have received less than their fair share of the material benefits of being American. In Europe, material benefits devolve increasingly from belonging to the European Community as a whole rather than from being part of Britain or Belgium or France.

Political authorities have never found it easy to live with their subjects' multilayered identities. Ancient texts testify to this difficulty:

> Then Haman said to King Ahasuerus, "There is a certain people, dispersed among the many peoples in all the provinces of your kingdom, who keep themselves apart. Their laws are different from those of every other people; they do not keep your majesty's laws. It does not befit your majesty to tolerate them."[16]

Haman ended up on the gallows, but his fate did not deter absolutists in subsequent generations, from seventeenth-century France ("one king, one law, one faith") to the First World War-era United States ("100 per cent Americanism") to today's Burma ("true Burmese are Buddhists"). If globalization is to have a positive cultural effect, it will be in encouraging and perhaps even forcing people to see beyond reductionist slogans of this sort. If they do not, more Bosnias will be the likely result. One necessary element in preventing more Bosnias will be to give recognition, at times even political recognition, to the complexity of culture and identity.

The map of a globalized world will not be drawn in one undifferentiated colour, but it will not be the familiar neat and discrete patches of pink, orange, yellow and green either. Mapmakers will need to learn to portray levels, overlaps and interpenetrations, the same ones the rest of us will need to learn to live with.

Canada: Cultures and Contracts

There is a duality in the modern idea of the nation, betraying its dual origin in eighteenth-century Enlightenment humanism and nineteenth-century German romanticism. At their extremes, one camp sees the nation as a collection of individuals who come together willingly in a social contract (the original meaning of this term should not be obscured by its use in Ontario in 1993 to describe government-imposed wage and job cuts), while the other sees the nation as an organic unity bonded by a common ancestry, culture and traditions. Sociologist J. Yvon Thériault of the University of Ottawa calls these two concepts *nation-contrat* and *nation-culture*: contractual nation and cultural nation.[17] Most nations in the modern world contain elements of both, and ideally maintain a healthy tension between them; it is that tension, in fact, that prevents them from collapsing into Jihad on the one hand or being absorbed into McWorld on the other.

If no nation is purely contractual or purely cultural, Canada leans heavily towards the contractual side of the continuum. In English Canada, to the extent that people identify distinctive and unifying elements in the country's "culture," they more often than not have to do with its *political* culture — Red Toryism, social programs, the CCF, the CBC. Just to list these elements is to take the measure of how precarious this political culture is in the 1990s. Thus, the presence of CBC television in Canada's cultural life was considerable when it was the only television available, as it was in the 1950s, or when it was one of a half-dozen or so channels, as it was in the 1960s. It is rather less so when it is one of 500 or more channels, as it may be in the late 1990s. Mark Starowicz, the CBC's head of documentaries, writes:

> The conundrum of Canadian national culture will be resolved with the brutality of a highway collision within this decade. The 1,000-channel universe and the infinity of choices that is coming upon us with the amalgam of the computer, digitalization and satellite compression will leave us naked. Either we will learn to compete on the playing field of CD-ROMs that contain entire encyclopedias, produce the films that assert our existence in the electronic video libraries that will dominate our lives, and develop Canadian international satellite channels, or we will be the victims of the age of the satellite and digitalization.[18]

Technological developments are also eroding the rules favouring Canadian magazine publishers that have encouraged the growth of a Canadian magazine industry. These rules, designed to prevent "split runs" or magazines with Canadian advertising but largely foreign editorial content, were drawn up in the 1960s and 1970s and were to be enforced by stopping magazines at the border — something that is difficult to do in the era of electronic page transmission. Time Warner's *Sports Illustrated* took advantage of this technological breach in Canada's walls to begin publishing a split-run edition in April 1993. *Sports Illustrated Canada* gave itself a Canadian face by paying particular attention to Canadian-based professional teams in thoroughly continentalized sports such as hockey and baseball; the result was about as culturally distinctive as, say, a special Pittsburgh edition that paid particular attention to the Pirates, Penguins and Steelers might be.

These technological changes pose especially difficult questions for Canada because most of the elements of Canadians' core culture have tended to be defined in units that are either smaller or larger than the contractual nation of Canada — the British Empire, North America, Quebec, Newfoundland, the Cree Nation. As Canada moves towards larger economic units and Ottawa abdicates much of its remaining economic power, the terms of the contract between Canada and its people change. It is not surprising that accommodating this change should be more difficult in Canada than in countries where the cultural nation plays a larger role. Even if France cedes political and economic power to European institutions, there is still deep meaning in being French. However, if the political and economic authority of the government of Canada is reduced, it is far less clear what significance remains to the term "Canadian." This is perhaps why English Canadians, at least, have tended to express support for the idea of a "strong central government," even if no one is quite sure just what this government should do or indeed whether it can effectively do much of anything.

We suggested earlier that the weakening of the nation-state and other effects of globalization have brought with them new forms of identity politics, competitive victimology and an unprecedented questioning of the superiority of Western culture. In Canada, the issues surrounding these developments have been especially intractable, as was manifested again in the negotiations leading to the Charlottetown constitutional agreement and the referendum campaign of 1992.

For if Canada is an essentially contractual nation, it contains within it nations with a much larger cultural component, notably the aboriginal nations and the Québécois. The cultural unity of French Quebecers is reinforced by a sense of historical grievance dating back to 1763. They entered the Charlottetown episode with the view that their victimization had been reaffirmed by the unilateral repatriation of the constitution in 1982 and the failure of the attempt at reconciliation embodied in the Meech Lake Accord in 1990. But this time they were not to be the only ones seeking to redress a longstanding historical wrong.

Elijah Harper's "No" to Meech Lake in June 1990 and the subsequent standoff at Oka signalled to Canadians that to solve their constitutional problems they would have to come to some accommodation with the aboriginal nations with whom they share Canadian territory. As these issues developed through the early 1990s, they revealed the extent to which Canadian sovereignty over these nations was both legally ambiguous and deleterious to the people directly concerned.

An Inuit judge, James Igloliorte, ruling that Labrador Innu were not trespassing when they came onto Canadian Forces Base Goose Bay to protest low-level military flights "because of their honest belief that the land was theirs," noted that the Innu have never ceded their land to Canada. He continued:

> All of the legal reasonings are based on the premise that somehow the Crown acquired [the land] magically by its own declaration of title. It is time this premise based on seventeenth century reasoning be questioned in the light of twenty-first century reality. Canada is a vital part of the global village and must show its maturity not only to the segment of Canadian society that wields great power and authority . . . but also to its most desperate people.[19]

What is noteworthy in this judgement, which was overturned on appeal, is not only Igloliorte's acknowledgement of the Innu's right to the land but also his belief that Canada owed it to the international community to recognize that right. Questions of land rights and international responsibility, as well as environmental issues, also underlay the struggle between the Cree and Hydro-Quebec over the second phase of the James Bay hydroelectric project. In Manitoba, an inquiry into aboriginal justice recommended a separate aboriginal

justice system, arguing that it was a logical aspect of self-government, to which aboriginal people have an inherent right.

The terms of the debate were changing rapidly, and it was in this
context that the federal government released its new set of constitutional proposals in the fall of 1991. It included provisions for aboriginal self-government, but only as a "justiciable" rather than as an
"inherent" right. Meanwhile, Quebec was to have the status of a
"distinct society." There was much haggling over terminology, and
the aboriginal people obtained the insertion of the word "inherent"
into the eventual constitutional package, embodied in the Charlottetown Accord. What is important for our purposes, however, is that
all the terms under serious consideration reflected a much more
supple notion of sovereignty than the one incorporated into Pierre
Trudeau's constitutional revision of 1982.

But there were difficulties. Both Quebec and the aboriginal nations engaged in competitive victimology, each claiming that its
demands were more fundamental than the other's. Even though (or
perhaps because) the Charlottetown Accord contained efforts at accommodation for a wide variety of groups, those who did not consider themselves accommodated — notably women, and especially
aboriginal women — were firm in their opposition. Many Canadians
wondered what would become of their country if so many bits of
sovereignty were parcelled out, or were simply opposed to conceiv-
ing of sovereignty in anything other than absolute terms. And while
the Charlottetown Accord represented a consensus among a broader
range of leaders than Meech Lake or other previous constitutional
agreements, few of those leaders took adequate care to ensure that
the people they led were brought in on the deal. In the end, the accord
was rejected by the electorate; neither Quebec nor the aboriginal
nations nor most of the English-speaking provinces supported it.
Postmodern constitution-making turned out to be a more hazardous
process than the politicians had allowed for.

Unsure about what the No vote meant, politicians interpreted it as
a mandate to stop talking about the constitution altogether. The
country went on as before, except that it couldn't really go on as
before. During the referendum campaign federal ministers hinted at
the prospect of Canada's becoming like Yugoslavia or Lebanon if
the Charlottetown Accord were rejected. These comparisons were
widely and rightly considered odious and absurd. A more apt, and
certainly less depressing, analogy might be Czechoslovakia, which
broke into two nation-states without civil war at the end of 1992. It

could also still be hoped that Canadians would develop a political structure that would reflect the multiple and overlapping communities and cultural groups they were part of, but the evidence on which to base any such hope remained slim.

Meanwhile, by the summer of 1993, the cultural debate appeared to be attaining a certain maturity. In a major essay in *Foreign Affairs*, Harvard strategic studies professor Samuel P. Huntington argued that the world is entering a period in which the major divisions will be cultural rather than ideological. He identified eight major "civilizations" (Western, Confucian, Japanese, Islamic, Hindu, Slavic-Orthodox, Latin American, African), and suggested that the world's major conflicts will break out in the "fault lines" between those civilizations — as, for example, in the former Yugoslavia.[20]

In another article, *Harper's* contributing editor David Rieff drew a preliminary link between economic globalization and the changes demanded by advocates of multiculturalism. In his view, it is not multiculturalism but capitalism, "the bull in the china shop of human history," that will undermine the supremacy of Western civilization.[21] The ingrained habit of thinking about culture in primarily national terms is not likely to disappear overnight, but there is evidence that other ways of thinking about it are beginning to gain strength.

Chapter 8

Is Globalization Good?

The project of rethinking free trade and establishing an alternative agenda for a global economy needs to be carried out on several levels. First, it will be worthwhile for progressive critics of the prevailing corporate agenda, who (especially in Canada) have overwhelmingly opposed free trade, to ask whether it is free trade itself that is the problem or the particular forms it has taken and the purposes for which it has been used. Second, a clear distinction needs to be drawn between a global economy and the formation of regional trade blocs, which is only protectionism on a larger scale. Another clear distinction needs to be drawn between trade policy and social policy, so that free trade is not used as an excuse for regressive social measures. The idea that national governments have no role in a global economy does not stand up to serious examination, but just what their role ought to be needs clarification. And the possibilities of expanding globalization beyond the areas of trade and investment to include the environment, human rights, health and other concerns deserve to be explored.

The Less Unhappy Medium

Trade and competition bring better goods at lower prices; they also bring job losses, social disruption and widespread insecurity. Extreme laissez-faire conditions yield extreme results: slavery, terror and despotism. But put too many restraints on trade and you end up with depression and war. As usual, there has to be a happy medium (or, failing that, a less unhappy medium). But where do we find it?

Globalization as it is currently understood involves large multinational companies pulling strings in different parts of the globe with puppets dancing to produce whatever it is they can do most cheaply and efficiently. We are supposed to like this because it means that we as consumers get low-priced, varied and high-quality goods. How we fit in as workers and producers is more ambiguous. We are told we have to raise our productivity or lower our living standards. If investment decisions were taken purely on grounds of efficiency, we might be more approving. But investment does sometimes go where labour or environmental standards are close to nonexistent, where taxes can be avoided or evaded, or where businesses and governments offer each other the most extravagant bribes.

Just as property rights tend to favour those who own property, free trade tends to favour those who control the factors of trade. We allow this because it often makes for a more efficient use of resources. Even the pretence that centrally planned economies are a viable alternative to the play of market forces no longer exists. Since we do still exercise some degree of sovereignty over our national territory, we can insist that corporations obey at least some of our laws some of the time. Even so, we are told we have to be flexible for fear of scaring away investment and jobs. It is easy enough to point to the disproportionate amount of power wielded by corporations. It is more difficult to design an economy that can curb that power and still operate efficiently.

Some critics of free trade point to Canada's prolonged recession and say free trade with the U.S. has hampered economic growth. Other critics make just the opposite claim, stating that it will create too much economic growth and put heavier strains on the environment, especially if some of this growth is directed to countries where enforcement of environmental regulations tends to be lax. Mexico is the country mentioned most often, and the environmental argument then gets turned against Mexicans who are looking for jobs. Not many environmentalists would come out and say that they prefer to see more Mexicans jobless and living in poverty, but it is hard to provide more jobs without some form of economic growth. NAFTA, for its many faults, does at least offer the possibility of a closer monitoring of ecological concerns. And a prosperous country has more resources that can be devoted to environmental protection than a poor country. It is wrong to punish people in Mexico or other poor countries for a world environmental mess that is largely the making of people in the richer countries. Free trade is no environmentally neutral panacea, but neither is protectionism.

Multinational companies have provided much of the impetus for free trade, which is why some critics tend to regard trade liberalization as part of a corporate conspiracy. Let us merely point out that many of these same companies have provided the impetus for protectionism — for example countervailing duties on steel imports into the U.S. — and that protectionism remains a tool of corporate greed. It cuts both ways.

Free Trade or Retrenchment?

Notions of free trade are the product of boom times. Free trade is the result of the operation of the business cycle, not the cause of it. Free trade may extend the boom for a time in the most powerful economy. GATT was a product of American hegemony; when the United States ceased to be the world's only economic superpower, American enthusiasm for GATT waned.

Placed in this perspective, the heady talk of Europe 1992 was a phenomenon of the 1980s, as was the word that it was "morning in America" and that "Canada is open for business again." Our point is not to raise the ghost of clichés past but merely to suggest that the first rush of enthusiasm for globalization was a product of different times.

As we have seen, global trade is not something new. What is new is that several advanced powers are trying to establish a safe, secure domestic market while encouraging foreign trade. This goal, problematic in itself, is made still more so by the fact that they all make and trade the same products. Furthermore, in many cases the makers of these products are transnational corporations, and even when they are not, they operate within a single capital market. Thus, while it is possible to see the emergence of trading blocs in Europe and Asia (while the Japanese have so far resisted the idea of forming a bloc, they have moved as vigorously as anyone to secure their domestic market) as something akin to the competition for markets that preceded the First World War, the situation is somewhat more complicated in that the world is much more interconnected and the land rush that led to colonial rivalries a century ago has been largely transferred to a competition for market share on the home turf.

The evidence on the effects of the Canada-U.S. Free Trade Agreement on the Canadian economy may be somewhat murky, especially given the recession and restructuring that would have occurred with or without the FTA. In one area, however, the evidence is crystal clear. From the American point of view, the FTA does not represent free trade at all. The agreement has hampered Canada's economic relations with the rest of the world — and without providing the secure and preferential access to the American market Canadians thought they were getting. We believe that North American economic integration is reaching the point where it is only a matter of time before serious questions are raised about the continued viability of Canadian political independence. If Canada wants to avoid this path, its best option is a determined effort to diversify its economic relationships, and the most effective way to do this is to chop away at trade barriers with the rest of the world.

Money Isn't Everything

There is no generic link between trade and social policy. Where a connection does exist, most specifically in the effects of social spending on international competitiveness, countries favouring broad social programs are not always at a disadvantage.

In Canada we have become convinced that all we have left to define ourselves as a society is the tattered and torn medicare system, and if we don't cut our expectations even further to size we will lose that as well. However, Canada's relatively generous system of public financing costs less than the narrower U.S. system, giving firms operating in Canada a slight competitive advantage. That the existing health-care system is untenable has become apparent to just about everybody in the United States, including the corporate sector. In 1991, the Ford Motor Co., commenting on the difficulty of competing with imports, said that the lack of state medical care added $500 to the cost of every automobile produced in the U.S. And Quebec-based furniture maker Shermag Inc., to take merely one example, closed a plant it had purchased in Massachusetts because U.S. health insurance costs were too high. If the two countries' health-care systems are to be "harmonized," Americans are more likely to move towards a Canadian-style system than vice versa. Canada's health-care system may be in trouble, but this has less to do with free trade than with the fact that costs have grown more quickly than the economy supporting that system.

We asserted that social concerns should sometimes take precedence over economic concerns. Money makes the world go round, as the song used to say, but — we know you've heard it before — money isn't everything. What we think public policymakers should get away from is the pretence that all their decisions have to make economic sense. Some policies don't make economic sense but should be supported anyway if the social or cultural reasons are strong enough to outweigh the economic costs. And the people making those policies should have the courage to say so. We have argued that trade policy should not be used as an instrument of social policy

— a clear distinction is needed between the two — but neither should trade policy be used as an excuse for neglecting social needs.

Who Is in Charge?

One of many myths surrounding free trade is the notion that it means governments must retreat to their centuries-old role of raising armies while leaving the rest to the unhindered operation of market forces. We are told that the nation-state, that product of the nineteenth-century marketplace, is no longer effective in conducting, regulating or even protecting economic activity within its jurisdiction, and therefore has no role. At the same time, however, no alternative institution or form of governance has arisen. Hence the most powerful states have never been more active, taking on such far-reaching and basic tasks as the organization of a global economic system. In Canada, a government such as the ragtag group of Conservative MPs we have seen recently, which can pose and preen and put the world back together again at G-7 summits, comes home and cringes in terror over the bond rating to be issued as a result of its latest budget or financial statement.

Who is in charge? Is anybody?

Government remains a fundamental unanswered question of the modern global economy. What institution can direct and develop the whole range of social and cultural attributes of a modern society? These aspects of life seem lost in all the glib assertions of a global economic wave about to engulf the planet, beyond the control of any social organization or other expression of political will.

In the context of free trade, the need for public authorities with an economic as well as a social and cultural role is clear. The world's three biggest trading countries all pursue industrial strategies — Japan and Germany overtly and the U.S. through Defense Department contracts that often create civilian spinoffs. (Now that the Defense Department has less money to spend, the U.S. is becoming more sensitive to subsidies elsewhere, as the Boeing-Airbus dispute demonstrates.) Some countries, particularly in Asia, have pursued successful industrial strategies while others in several parts of the world have been abysmal failures. Arguments can be made for or against industrial strategies, but where the government's main role is one of instigator and coordinator, as in the Quebec government's incipient industrial strategy, not even the broadest definition of subsidy can be used to justify trade sanctions. Discussion papers issued by the Quebec government in 1992 urged a strategy based on more intensive development of existing industrial "clusters" in several key sectors. This strategy envisages cooperation between competing firms and also among these businesses, government departments and institutions of higher learning. But mention of subsidies is avoided.

Naturally the suspicion arises that governments are weak and irrelevant because the economic powers-that-be want them that way. If that were all that was involved, it would be relatively easy to correct the problem and reverse the process. But the world has changed, and the impotence of current institutions even to approach the really crucial global issues of stopping environmental degradation and creating balanced world development creates an aura of crisis. Even more local and mundane issues now seem insoluble within the strict jurisdictional confines of individual states. This is more apparent in smaller and weaker states such as Canada, but the same forces are at work in the major powers. Can the United States control the mass northern migration? Can Western Europe, acting as a unit or as individual countries, control the fallout from the collapse of the East?

If the old economic order is changing, yielding place to new, then new political structures will have to arise to reflect and organize this change. One cannot happen without the other.

Broadening Globalization

If globalization is limited to multinational corporations, it presents the prospect of power being concentrated in a collection of worldwide feudal baronies. If it is extended beyond that sphere to encompass the creation of genuinely global institutions, it offers the possibility of a more creative and effective approach to some of the most urgent problems facing the world: security, the environment, human rights. Proposals to broaden globalization in this way will not come from the corporations themselves. They must come from other sectors of society — trade unions, political parties of the centre and left, extraparliamentary coalitions, religious groups and nongovernmental organizations of various kinds.

In the past, these groups often failed to see beyond their own national borders. We noted that some preliminary steps towards overcoming that limitation of vision are now being taken — especially in the areas of the environment, human rights and health and even among some of the groups active in opposing the North American Free Trade Agreement. Building on these first efforts to develop an alternative global vision is the crucial challenge of the coming years.

Notes

Chapter 1: The New World Order and Canada's Place in It

1. Richard J. Barnet and Ronald E. Müller, *Global Reach: The Power of the Multinational Corporation* (New York: Simon and Schuster, 1974), p. 363.
2. Richard J. Barnet, "Reflections: The Disorders of Peace," *New Yorker*, January 20, 1992, p. 65.
3. Japan, although an economic giant, has never had the political, military and cultural power to be classified as a superpower.
4. See *Investor's Business Daily*, September 1993.
5. Richard Gwyn, Toronto *Star*, June 13, 1993.
6. Statistics Canad, cat. no. 65-003, 1988 and 1992.
7. Statistics Canada *Daily*, August 24, 1993; Statistics Canada cat. no. 65-003 and 65-006, 1989.
8. Michael Vlahos, *The National Interest*, Summer 1990.
9. Political activist Jesse Jackson and consumer rights advocate Ralph Nader are among those who have taken this position.

Chapter 2: How New Is Globalization?

1. See Eric Hobsbawm, *The Age of Capital* (New York: Charles Scribner's Sons, 1975), for the origin and usage of the term *capitalism*. The term comes into wide usage in the 1860s but its origins precede 1848.
2. Hobsbawm, *Age of Capital*, (New York: Charles Scribner's Sons, 1975), pp. 36-37.
3. Karl Marx and Friedrich Engels, *The Communist Manifesto*, in *Selected Works*, Vol. 1 (Moscow: foreign Languages Publishing House, 1962), p. 37.
4. *The Economist*, March 27, 1993.
5. See Paul Johnson, *Modern Times* (New York: Harper, 1991), for an interesting description of the workings of capitalism in prerevolutionary Russia.
6. *The Economist*, March 27, 1993.
7. Hobsbawm, *Age of Capital*, p. 167.
8. V.I. Lenin, *Critical Remarks on the National Question* (Moscow: Progress Publishers, 1951), p. 11.
9. Cited in Lenin, *Critical Remarks*, p. 12.
10. Lenin, *Critical Remarks*, pp. 13-14.
11. "Is opposing NAFTA in workers' interests?", *The Militant*, May 17, 1993, p. 10.
12. Robert S. McElvaine, *The Great Depression: America 1929-1941* (New York: Times Books, 1984), p. 82.
13. Cited in McElvaine, *Great Depression*, p. 82.
14. McElvaine, *Great Depression*, p. 84.
15. Peter F. Drucker, *Post-Capitalist Society* (New York: HarperBusiness, 1993).
16. Ibid., pp. 25-27.
17. See Bertrand Bellon and Jorge Niosi, *The Decline of the American Economy*, trans. Robert Chodos and Ellen Garmaise (Montreal: Black Rose, 1988), pp. 141-42.
18. John Kenneth Galbraith, *American Capitalism: The Concept of Countervailing Power* (Boston: Houghton Mifflin, 1952).
19. Quoted in Stephen E. Ambrose, *The Rise to Globalism: American Foreign Policy since 1938*, 5th ed. (New York: Penguin, 1988), pp. 79-80.
20. Paul Kennedy, *The Rise and Fall of the Great Powers* (New York: Random House, 1987), p. 241.
21. The Senator Gravel Edition, *The Pentagon Papers: The Defense Department History of Decisionmaking on Vietnam*, vol. 1 (Boston: Beacon, 1971), pp. 385-86. The policy of creating Japan as a bulwark against China is developed in several studies of that period, notably Herbert S. Parmet, *Richard Nixon and His America* (Boston: Little, Brown, 1990).

22. Kantor's testimony before the Senate Committee confirming his appointment as U.S. Trade Representative. Robert Heilbroner, "Capitalism's Last Stand," *Report on Business* magazine, May 1993, p. 37.
23. See Howard M. Wachtel, *The Money Mandarins: The Making of a Supranational Economic Order* (New York: Pantheon, 1986), pp. 104-9, 175-78.
24. Estimates from a table compiled by sociologist François Moreau of the University of Ottawa from International Monetary Fund and Bank for International Settlements sources and published in *Mondialisation et régionalisation: La coopération économique internationale est-elle encore possible?*, edited by Christian Deblock and Diane Éthier (Quebec: Presses de l'Université du Québec, 1992), p. 255.
25. Bernard Élie, "L'évolution du système financier international et son impact dans les années 90," in *Mondialisation et régionalisation*, edited by Deblock and Éthier, p. 226.
26. Roy C. Smith, *The Global Bankers* (New York: Truman Talley Books/Plume, 1989), pp. 66-67.
27. See David Marsh, *The Bundesbank: The Bank that Rules Europe* (London: William Heinemann, 1992).
28. Howard M. Wachtel, *The Money Mandarins: The Making of a Supranational Economic Order* (New York: Pantheon, 1986), p. 183.
29. See, for example, Robert Heilbroner and Peter Bernstein, *The Debt and the Deficit: False Alarms/Real Possibilities* (New York: W.W. Norton, 1989), pp. 21-27.
30. Galbraith discusses this problem with Marxism in several of his works, perhaps most eloquently in the television series and book *The Age of Uncertainty* (Boston: Houghton Mifflin, 1977).
31. Drucker, *Post-Capitalist Society*.
32. Robert Heilbroner, "Capitalism's Last Stand," *Report on Business* magazine, May 1993.
33. *The Economist*, October 26, 1991.
34. Walter Stewart, *Uneasy Lies the Head: The Truth about Canada's Crown Corporations* (Toronto: Collins, 1987).

Chapter 3: Globalization versus the Nation-State

1. Clive Crook, "All Systems Slow," *The Economist*, March 27, 1993.
2. *The Economist* and *Report on Business* magazine, joint issue, January 1993.
3. Clyde V. Prestowitz, Jr., Alan Tonelson and Robert W. Jerone, "The Last Gasp of Gattism," *Harvard Business Review*, March-April 1991, excerpted in *World Politics: Annual Edition 1992-93* (Guilford, Conn.: Dushkin Publishing Group, 1992), p. 181.
4. Robert Kuttner, *The End of Laissez-Faire: National Purpose and the Global Economy after the Cold War* (New York: Alfred A. Knopf, 1992).
5. Arthur M. Schlesinger, Jr., *The Cycles of American History* (Boston: Houghton Mifflin, 1986).
6. "Japanese Shifting Investment Flow Back toward Home," New York *Times*, March 22, 1992.
7. Martin Wollacott, "Stop the World While We All Get Off," Manchester *Guardian*, March 7, 1993.
8. There may be exceptions: the U.S. and Israel, for example, or some of the arrangements between Russia and its former satellites and its eastern republics.
9. *The Economist*, February 6, 1993.
10. Toronto *Globe and Mail*, February 17, 1993.
11. Gilles Paquet, "État postmoderne: mode d'emploi," *Relations*, January-February 1993, pp. 17-19.
12. *Business Week*, February 8, 1993, pp. 98-103.
13. Reginald Weiser, interview with one of the authors, April 23, 1993.
14. James Laxer, "A New Look at Canadian Water: Sovereignty Is Not the Best Argument for Resisting Water Diversion," *Compass*, July/August 1992, p. 8.
15. Walter Russell Mead, "Bushism, Found: A Second-Term Agenda Hidden in Trade Agreements," *Harper's*, September 1992, pp. 37-45.
16. Public Citizen's Congress Watch, "The Tuna-Dolphin GATT Decision," in *Everything You Always Wanted to Know about GATT, but Were Afraid to Ask* (Washington,

1991); David Phillips (Earth Island Institute), "Statement on the Implications of the GATT Panel Ruling on Dolphin Protection and the Environment before the Subcommittee on Health and the Environment of the House Energy and Commerce Committee," September 27, 1991; Eric Christensen, "GATT Nets an Environmental Disaster: A Legal Analysis and Critique of the GATT Panel Ruling on Imports of Mexican Yellowfin Tuna into the United States" (Washington: Community Nutrition Institute, 1991).

17. Public Citizen's Congress Watch, "The Dolphin Case is Just One of Many," in *Everything You Always Wanted to Know about GATT.*

18. See "Mothers' Milk Threatened by Free Trade Pact," *INFACT Canada Newsletter,* Fall 1991, p. 1, and Elisabeth Sterken, "Formula Companies' Miracle Cure," *This Magazine,* June–July 1993, p. 9.

19. Sterken, "Formula Companies' Miracle Cure."

20. WHO and UNICEF estimate that a million and a half infant deaths could be averted each year through effective breastfeeding.

21. At a Codex Alimentarius meeting in Geneva in July 1989, for example, Nestlé representatives sat on the Swiss, French, German, British and Belgian delegations. The U.S. delegation included representatives of Mead Johnson, Wyeth-Ayerst and Kraft.

22. World Commission on Environment and Development, *Our Common Future* (Oxford: At the University Press, 1987).

23. "NGO Debt Treaty," in *Alternative Treaty-Making Process, Section C: Alternative Economic Issues,* prepublication edition, October 1992, p. C-13.

24. Irwin Cotler, "Human Rights as the Modern Tool of Revolution," in *Human Rights in the Twenty-First Century: A Global Challenge,* ed. Kathleen E. Mahoney and Paul Mahoney (Dordrecht, The Netherlands: Martinus Nijhoff, 1993), p. 14.

Chapter 4: The Growth of Trade Blocs

1. James C. Hathaway, "Harmonizing for Whom?: The Devaluation of Refugee Protection in the Era of Regional Economic Integration," *Cornell International Law Journal,* Spring 1993. See also Hans Magnus Enzenberger, "The Great Migration," tr. Martin Chalmers, *Granta,* Winter 1992, pp. 15-51.

2. James Laxer, *Inventing Europe: The Rise of a New World Power* (Toronto: Lester Publishing, 1991), p. 150.

3. Ibid., p. 152.

4. *The Economist,* February 6, 1993.

5. Ibid. This fact was verified by the then-president of Hoover Europe, William Foust. Foust, however, has difficulty with figures, as he was later to approve a marketing gimmick where a customer could receive a return air trip to America for the purchase of a small vacuum cleaner. While the American headquarters now has to cope with millions of dollars in air fares, a new president of Hoover Europe has to deal with a market suddenly awash in second-hand vacuum cleaners.

6. *Newsweek,* December 16, 1991.

7. Helmut Schmidt, "Birth of a Multination, Maybe," New York *Times,* December 8, 1991.

8. James Laxer, *False God: How the Globalization Myth Has Impoverished Canada* (Toronto: Lester Publishing, 1993). See especially chapter 3.

9. Greenpeace Québec, "L'accord du libre échange nord américain: Vivent les multinationales," *Le Monde à Bicyclette,* Montreal, Summer 1993.

10. *Mexico: A Travel Survival Kit* (Melbourne: Lonely Planet Publications, 1989), p. 707.

11. Ibid., p. 843.

12. Statistics Canada, *Exports by Country,* cat. 65-003, and *Imports by Country,* cat. 65-006 (Ottawa, March 1993).

13. Interview with one of the authors, April 28, 1993.

14. José Angel Conchello, *El TLC: un callejón sin salida* (Mexico City: Editorial Grijalbo, 1992).

15. Jorge G. Castañeda and Carlos Heredia, "Hacia otro TLC," *Nexos,* January 1993, pp. 43-54.

16. Edward Broadbent, "Human Rights and the North American Free Trade Agreement," acceptance speech for the Human Rights Award, B'nai B'rith Hillel Foundation, March 23, 1992.
17. Jagdish Bhagwati, *Regionalism and Multilateralism: An Overview,* discussion paper no. 603 (New York: Columbia University Department of Economics, 1992), pp. 37-38.
18. Ibid., p. 38.

Chapter 5: One World or Three?

1. John J. Mearsheimer, "Why We Will Soon Miss the Cold War," *Atlantic Monthly,* August 1990, excerpted in *Taking Sides: Third Edition* (Guilford, Conn.: Dushkin Publishing Group, 1991), p. 13.
2. *The Economist,* January 11, 1992.
3. Toronto *Globe and Mail,* March 3, 1993.
4. Walter Russell Mead, "On the Road to Ruin," *Harper's,* March 1990, pp. 60-64.
5. Lester Thurow, speech in Toronto, quoted in the Toronto *Star,* January 28, 1993.
6. Ibid.
7. George Will, syndicated column, St. Petersburg *Times,* February 2, 1993.
8. Francis Fukuyama, "The End of History," *The National Interest,* Summer 1989.
9. Charles Krauthammer, "The Unipolar Moment," *Foreign Affairs,* vol. 70, no. 1 (winter 1991), excerpted in *Taking Sides: Fourth Edition* (Guilford, Conn.: Dushkin Publishing Group, 1992), p. 38.
10. Paul Kennedy, *The Rise and Fall of the Great Powers* (New York: Random House, 1987).
11. Toronto *Globe and Mail,* April 1, 1993.
12. Toronto *Star,* April 4, 1993.
13. Clyde V. Prestowitz, Jr., Alan Tonelson and Robert W. Jerone, "The Last Gasp of Gattism," *Harvard Business Review,* March-April 1991, excerpted in *World Politics: Annual Edition 1992-93* (Guilford, Conn.: Dushkin Publishing Group, 1992).
14. Murray Weidenbaum, *Washington Quarterly,* vol. 15, number 1 (Winter 1992).
15. Richard J. Barnet, "Reflections: The Disorders of Peace," *New Yorker,* January 20, 1992, p. 65.
16. Michael Vlahos, *The National Interest,* summer 1990, excerpted in *World Politics: Annual Edition 1992-93* (Guilford, Conn.: Dushkin Publishing Group, 1992), p. 173.
17. See Statistics Canada, Exports by Country, Cat. 65-003, March 1989 and March 1993.
18. *Financial Times of Canada,* February 27, 1993.
19. Toronto *Globe and Mail,* March 1, 1993.
20. International Trade Minister Michael Wilson, Toronto *Globe and Mail,* August 4, 1992.
21. Richard Gwyn, Toronto *Star,* February 25, 1993. This is quoted not only because it was typical of Mulroney's resignation responses but also for its careless interpretation of part of the trade statistics — which was also typical of the week's news.
22. Desmond Morton, *A Short History of Canada* (Edmonton: Hurtig, 1983) p. 142.
23. *The Economist,* February 27, 1993.
24. Toronto *Star,* February 7, 1993.
25. *The Economist,* March 13, 1993.

Chapter 6: Four Key Industries

1. Carl E. Beigie, *The Canada-U.S. Automotive Agreement: An Evaluation* (Washington: National Planning Association/Montreal: Private Planning Association of Canada, 1970).
2. There are small assembly plants as well as component producers for various Asian and European manufacturers, but there are minor and at the moment embattled players in the general scheme of the industry.
3. Joseph Schull, *Ontario Since 1867* (Toronto: McClelland and Stewart, 1978).
4. Lester Thurow, *Head to Head* (New York: William Morrow, 1992), pp. 114-15.
5. Toronto *Star,* May 5, 1993.

6. A detailed discussion of these negotiations is contained in Robert Reich and John Donahue, *New Deals: The Chrysler Revival and the American System* (New York: Penguin, 1985).
7. *The Economist*, May 2, 1993.
8. See Giles Gherson, *Financial Times of Canada*, April 10, 1993.
9. See "The Deal Is Offered," editorial, Toronto *Globe and Mail*, February 25, 1988.
10. *Financial Times of Canada*, April 10, 1992.
11. G. Bruce Doern and Brian W. Tomlin, *Faith and Fear: The Free Trade Story* (Toronto: Stoddart, 1991), pp. 93, 188-89, 251.
12. Giles Gherson, "A Bittersweet Lesson in Canada-U.S. Trade," *Financial Times of Canada*, August 3, 1992.
13. Ibid.
14. Terence Corcoran, "Get Tougher with U.S. on Trade," Toronto *Globe and Mail*, April 3, 1993.
15. Figures on agricultural subsidies mentioned here and in the following paragraph were compiled by the Organization for Economic Cooperation and Development and presented on page 4 of "Grotesque: A Survey of Agriculture," *The Economist*, December 12, 1992.

Chapter 7: Culture, Identity and the Nation-State

1. Jan Morris, "History Still Stirring Up Trouble in This Land of Rugby and Poets," Toronto *Globe and Mail*, November 28, 1992.
2. Benjamin R. Barber, "Jihad Vs. McWorld," *Atlantic Monthly*, March 1992, pp. 53-65.
3. Uwe Pörksen, *Plastikwörter: Die Sprache einer internationalen Diktatur* (Stuttgart: Klett-Cotta, 1988). An excerpt appeared in English as "From 5,000 Languages to 15 Words," *Compass*, July/August 1992, pp. 16-17.
4. See Robert Drinan SJ, Jan Stuyt SJ and Michael Czerny SJ, "World Conference on Human Rights," background paper (Rome, 1993).
5. Pörksen, "From 5,000 Languages to 15 Words," p. 17.
6. Arthur M. Schlesinger, Jr., *The Disuniting of America: Reflections on a Multicultural Society* (Knoxville, Tenn.: Whittle Direct Books, 1991).
7. See especially "Bless'd Be the Ties that Bind," *The Economist*, October 26, 1991, pp. 19-22.
8. Thomas Berger, *A Long and Terrible Shadow: White Values, Native Rights in the Americas 1492–1992* (Vancouver: Douglas and McIntyre, 1991); Ronald Wright, *Stolen Continents: The New World through Indian Eyes since 1492* (Toronto: Viking, 1992).
9. "Commemorating 1492" (Roundtable), *Tikkun*, September/October 1992, p. 58.
10. See, for example, "African Dreams," *Newsweek*, September 23, 1991, pp. 42-50.
11. Shelby Steele, "The New Sovereignty," *Harper's*, July 1992, p. 48.
12. George F. Will, "Literary Politics," *Newsweek*, April 22, 1991, p. 72.
13. These are 1991 census figures from Canada, Statistics Canada, *Ethnic Origin: The Nation*, cat. no. 93-315.
14. Charles C. Mann, "How Many Is Too Many?", *Atlantic Monthly*, February 1993, p. 66.
15. The persistence of this debate is evocatively and humorously portrayed in the 1991 film *Secret Nation*.
16. Esther 3:8 (New English Bible).
17. J. Yvon Thériault, "Les mouvements ethno-culturels," in *L'ethnicité à l'heure de la mondialisation*, edited by Caroline Andrew, Linda Cardinal, François Houle and Gilles Paquet (Ottawa: ACFAS-Outaouais, 1992), pp. 5-20.
18. Mark Starowicz, "Orchestra in the Parlor or Street-Corner Band?", *Compass*, July/August 1993, p. 35.
19. See Marie Wadden, "The Labrador Innu's Spring of Discontent," *This Magazine*, August 1990, p. 6.
20. Samuel P. Huntington, "The Clash of Civilizations?," *Foreign Affairs*, Summer 1993, pp. 22-49.
21. David Rieff, "Multiculturalism's Silent Partner: It's the Newly Globalized Consumer Economy, Stupid," *Harper's*, August 1993, pp. 62-72.

Index